CW01666638

This book is a gift

....

Given to

....

By me

....

On this date

....

I gave you this gift because

....

....

RAISED BY MAMA, BUILT BY ABBA

Adediwura Arowosegbe

DEDICATION

To ABBA Father, my heavenly Father who sought for me and brought me into His love long before I knew what it meant to have a father. Your everlasting love is greater than life itself.

ACKNOWLEDGMENTS

I feel deeply honored and blessed to do life and complete this work with super amazing people on this side of eternity. I am super blessed to have you all and you deserve the very best!

I am one of five women in an amazing cocoon of love. I am forever grateful that God planted me among four wonderful women: my mom and three sisters. Thank you, mom, for encouraging me in my wildest dream and for your love from a pure heart. Thank you for leading me God's way even when my mind couldn't grasp it.

Adeyemi, thank you for your love. You are that sister everyone should have. Temitope, thank you for supplying me super 'bottom powers' when I needed it. Thank you for always going an extra mile for me, Ifeoluwa. I'm thankful that you all hold me dearly in your thoughts and I'm proud of the women you are.

Thank you for your prayers Dad, Mr. Solomon Arowosegbe. They are always a blessing. I'm thankful for the brothers I've gained in Papa Nini and Pastor Dayo. Nifemi and Ara, my treasured nephew and niece, every single time you looked into my face has made this journey richer in ways words cannot describe.

To my father-in-Christ, Pastor Paul Kinto, thank you for leading me on the journey to knowing God for myself. You are my angel!

Dearest Lady Debola Deji-Kurunmi (DDK), I prayed for a mentor, I got even more. Thank you for your contributions to the success of this book. I am thankful for the heart-warming conversations that helped me see, first through your life, the possibilities ahead of me as a Future Forward Woman.

To my super coach and brother-in-Christ, Dr. Samuel Ekundayo, getting on life's journey with your guidance is divinely ordained. The burden for this book was roused in your 'corner'. Thank you for believing in me. May I always make you prouder than you desire.

Sisterhood is indeed a golden thread to the meaning of life. I appreciate my sisters-in-Christ, my prayer partners, and firelighters. Thank you Bunmi Oduah for all you do. Aziz Temitope, Ugochi Obidiegwu, Oladayo Bode-Balogun, and Tosin Yemi-Sanni; thank you for your immense support. Adenike and Olanike, my beloved Worcester sisters, thank you for all you do.

To the Future Forward Women of the Immerse Inner Circle, thank you for spurring me unto greatness. Your energy is so divine. I enjoy doing life with you.

To the RCCG (Redeemed Christian Church of God) Power Miracle Center family, thank you for being an amazing part of this season of my life.

I love you all.

CONTENTS

FOREWORD

Adediwura, a woman I have come to love and greatly admire, has written a masterpiece, told with vulnerability, truth, and heart-warming hope.

The Book, *Raised by Mama, Built by Abba,* is a compelling journey of love, pain, healing, and promise. Whether or not you were raised by a single parent, you'd find yourself right in the pages somewhere, because this is OUR story!

Told from both the lens of a young girl and a mature woman, Wura takes us on the journey of a daughter longing for her absent father's love. You may cry as you read some scenes in this truly evocative plot, but you'd smile too - as your heartstrings are pulled into the ever-loving presence of Abba, the Dad who never fails! You'd be greatly inspired by the path she takes to navigate rejection, grow her gifts, preserve virtue, and triumph over the challenges of youth.

In sharing her own story, the author makes a case for healthy families and the impact of parenting on wholesome child development. Yet for anyone from a "dysfunctional" family, there is hope - as this is a rich collection of wisdom to make the most of what you've been given.

You'd learn to discern your own identity, choose love over loss, overcome disadvantaged conditioning, and build a love relationship with God, the Father!

I thank Adediwura for the brilliance of thought, simplicity of storytelling, heartfelt kindness, and honesty that shine through in this book. My desire is for every reader to utilize this transformational tool with attention and intention! It will change your life.
May the Blessings of Christ rest upon your spirit.

Debola Deji-Kurunmi
Ministry Gift, Coach, Public Policy Analyst and Author

PRAISE FOR RAISED BY MAMA, BUILT BY ABBA

Once in a while, you stumble upon a book that is written from the heart. You know it is written from the heart because it tugs at your heart as you flip through the pages. This book is one of those books written from the heart.

In *Raised by Mama, Built by Abba,* we are introduced into the world of a young African girl growing up in a home without a father. We feel her pain and her low moments as she tries to navigate a world that views her as broken, just because she comes from a broken home. But we are also inspired by her resilience and her depth of wisdom, as she talks about her relationship with the ultimate father - Abba Father.

I have the feeling that this would not be the last time we would be reading from this writer.

-Pastor Emeka Godwin
RCCG-PMC Worcester

"One of the biggest blows life throws at a young person is the absence of a nurturing environment to grow in, especially when it comes to having two committed parents in the home."

This was one of the statements that first got my attention in this masterpiece of a book. Amidst a myriad of troubles that could hit a person's life, the absence of love from one or both parents is one of the greatest. While the young and naive mind may not be able to interpret and fathom the immediate implication, it is only a matter of time before the void would hit and the realization would sink, deep like a drowning weight.

In such an unideal crucible one thing is certain, God never leaves His own. God never forsakes, even when parents leave or fail, God neither leaves nor fails so He is always there. This book relays God's role in filling the void left by such tragedy. God, as fond of Him, makes a way where there seems to be no way, builds the life of such people using men and women, resources in heaven and on earth, situations and circumstances, principles and miracles, law and grace, and everything in-between! *Raised by Mama, Built by Abba* is an account of God's love at work in the life of the seeming forsaken and unloved. Through the narratives of the author, we can experience and position ourselves in the victory that is possible when we allow God to build our lives the right way and make them beautiful.

-Dr. Samuel Ekundayo

The Purpose Preacher

Despite being part of the process as her book writing coach, I must confess that I was still pleasantly taken aback when I read Adediwura's manuscript for the first time. If you attend parties in Lagos, you can guess how great jollof rice will taste from the aroma as servers move with it from table to table. But there are times when you take a bite, it goes exceedingly, abundantly above all you could have ever imagined. That's how I felt about this book.

I knew it would be good, but my God! It turned out better. My only regret was that I read it in soft copy, and as a result, I couldn't underline the very many gems Adediwura so effortlessly shares as she masterfully tells this very inspiring story.

I love everything about this book. And you will too. Everyone should read *Raised by Mama, Built by Abba* with their seatbelts on, the book in one hand, and a pen in another. You won't be the same after this ride.

- Laju Iren
The Lord's Storyteller

I have enjoyed reading the book from a psycho-emotional perspective and I would like to say that the author did a great job communicating the negative impact of an absent father on the psychological wellbeing of a girl child. Such negative impact could be in form of depression, suicide, eating disorders, obesity, early sexual activity, addiction-formation, and difficulty building and holding on to loving relationships are all side-effects of an absent father.

The question is, how can a girl address her psycho-emotional issues without blaming her absent dad? I would like to encourage you to get a copy of the book to find out more.

Thank you, Adediwura, for blessing our world with this timely book. I am confident it will help many girls who grew up with an absent father heal from the hurt by embracing the unconditional love and resources of Abba.

-Dr. Adesayo Adelowo
Speaker, Coach, Author

In life, there are hurdles to jump. The absence of one parent doesn't deny their existence. *Raised by Mama, built by Abba* speaks to the depth of our existence and core values that need to be instilled in our childhood. When you find God early, regardless of your age, God will reveal Himself in the dimension of your void. Adediwura found God, stayed committed to Him, then the shift began. It is only God that can fix a broken heart. This is a story of a woman and her journey: her truth, her voice.

-Temitope Aziz

Author, Motherhood Confessions from Conception to Childbirth

Raised by Mama, Built by Abba is a journey that many of us can relate to in varied circumstances. This book is not intended to just explore and relive our painful past, it is rather focused on ensuring that we understand where we have been hurt and take steps towards purposeful healing so that we can fully live as God intended in every area of life.

While the way forward is not looking backward, it is not also shutting out the past. As individuals who have been affected and even societies, we must take cues that would help us unlearn, learn, and re-learn so that we don't become or remain victims of our past.

I believe and pray that many would find true healing and liberation as they read knowing that their journey is not unique to them.

Thank you, Dr. Adediwura, for this amazing book.

Oladayo Bode-Balogun

INTRODUCTION

When Is Dad Coming Back?

"When my father and my mother forsake me, then the LORD will take me up" Psalm 27:10

"What do I write?" I asked. I'm not sure where the idea came from, but mom had just asked that we write a letter to my 'long unseen' dad. Weeks had run into months and now, it had been a few years that he had been away. What do I say or ask? Should I ask why he has been away for so long? Or where he was at the moment? If he missed us? Should I tell him about all the things going on at school?

Several thoughts ran through my mind and I just couldn't decide which was most important given the limited space on the blank sheet I had before me. Beyond my constraints with space and limitless thoughts, another thought lingered long enough that I had to blurt out. "Does it really matter? Would it change anything?" I asked. "Just write something," my mom responded.

Those were the scenes playing in my mind as an eleven-year-old girl. While many were enjoying their moments with their parents and bonding as much as possible, I was coming to terms with my dad's absence and the possibility of growing in his absence. It probably didn't matter much at this point; I had already gotten used to it.

Over the years, as I left home to start college and especially as I settled into my womanhood and began to develop a sense of independence and individuality, I realized that my situation growing up was more common than I would have imagined— a good number of people in society today were raised without one or both parents, and most commonly without a dad. Many are still in the process. Is that something we need to take a pause and talk about? You may say yes, or maybe an outright no.

"You too", I have always said in dismay as more friends and acquaintances shared similar experiences. As I listened to them, I found myself wondering how they survived the storms, or if they did at all.
Sometimes, I ask questions to know what it meant to them and how it had shaped their lives. I can tell you that so far, I have gotten myriads of responses, some

unsurprising, others a call for concern, and some others are frightening.

Well, life is not fair, they say! One of the biggest blows life can throw at a young person is the absence of a nurturing environment to grow in, especially when it comes to having two committed parents in the home. As I experienced, different circumstances such as deaths, divorces, separations, 'disappearances', and birth by an unmarried mother feed us the unpleasant pill of growing up in the absence of one or both parents.

Living without one or both parents is a journey many don't talk about until their older successful years—usually when their successes are big enough to overshadow their childhood experiences. Even at that point, many still recount their story believing their journey may have been easier if they had both parents. Regardless of how awesome a single parent was, many wish they had a second great one in their daily lives too.

While there is never a storm-free journey through life, experiencing life as an orphan or as a child from a broken home comes with its unique challenges and disadvantages, big or small hurts, feelings of rejection,

money issues, poorer life outcomes; we have a whole world of worries to deal with.
Where do we go from here? What do we do with the hurts and our feelings of helplessness? Are we forever at the mercy of the brokenness of our homes? Can we ever rise beyond those limitations set for us very early in life? How do we navigate through our storm-tossed backgrounds and build the lives God desires for us?

Raised by Mama, Built by Abba is my story of finding love, hope, and strength during my childhood and teenage years. I have learned valuable lessons from my heavenly Father on how He loves and builds beautiful lives irrespective of backgrounds or disadvantages.
And while many spend years ignoring the pain and bearing enormous burdens from such experiences, I have learned to ride on this love, hope, strength, and support: I have found to be true His words *"Though thy father and mother forsake thee, I will never forsake thee."*

This book is not only intended to address our headaches and heartaches as we try to understand our 'different' situation. It acknowledges that a great family background is a super catalyst for a growing child. It also recognizes that having one or two constraints in our families does not prevent us from living God's intended best for our lives.

My desire for everyone to experience a richer beautiful life irrespective of their upbringing is perhaps my biggest motivation for writing this book. I pray that anyone lost, broken, or hurt by the homes or circumstances they grew in will find true healing; that families will find wholeness and oneness; and that we all will come to know and experience the wonderful life God has in mind for us, great family or not.

I hope that by reading this book, you become more convinced that God builds beautiful lives regardless of constraints or background; that it is possible to have the beautiful life God has mapped out for us, become what we always wanted to be, and reach our highest expectations. In the end, it would not matter anymore whether we were raised by one, two, many, or none at all.

CHAPTER ONE

MOM OR DAD; WHOSE SIDE AM I ON?

LOVE FROM TWO ENDS

Love matters. We all want love, we all need love. Everyone—old or young—desires to be loved. Everyone blossoms with a good and healthy dose of love. If there was any place I experienced love, it was first in my home; with my parents and siblings. While the concept of love was sparsely touched by my very traditional parents, their actions told a story their mouths did not. The few memories I have of my very early childhood are mostly lovey-dovey moments.

First, it was all the care and warmth I had. While my parents did not belong to the rich class, I don't seem to remember bad moments where I lacked the basic needs in my very early years. I also remember how much bond I shared with my siblings. I remember how we all gathered around and bonded with my last sister. We would always take turns to wrap her up in her shawl even when she had outgrown it.

Beyond the affections that my parents showed, a few of their actions undeniably spelled love. My seventh birthday was a very remarkable one. The week had been a great one. Finally, my dad arrived from work that weekend with a birthday card. It was beautiful in every sense of the word. It had very beautiful colors and a nice design. It had gold fonts too!

As you can already expect, my heart was charmed. I had never seen anything so beautiful. It meant that I was precious to have received such a gift, more like a princess. I was my daddy's girl. I treated the card as a priceless possession. My mom had it fixed on a part of our glass shelf. So, I got to see it often.

About the same time, I fell and had a big cut on my forehead while trying to climb up the stairs. We had just moved into a new apartment and I was yet to master my way around the house. I started bleeding and also went into a shock. Next thing, I was in a hospital getting my forehead stitched.

Then, I saw my mom in a state I had never witnessed before. All worried and concerned. Really? Was she really this much bothered if something happened to me? That moment, I knew how much I mattered to her. I had neither been treated wrongly nor felt out of place before now, but this hit differently; the people around me cherish having me, I concluded.

A home is a beautiful place with lots of love. Experts say that every recipe for growing a healthy child calls for a large serving of love. When we are very young, our desire for love is supplied in all those thousands of interactions we experience with the people around us, especially in our homes. I believe I got a good dose in my early years.

And borrowing the Canadian children's singer Raffi's lyrics to express my early years:

"I had a song in my heart, food in my belly and love in my family … and I had clean water for drinking, and some clean air for breathing."

Dad and mom had a very memorable wedding ceremony—picture perfect. The pictures tell a coherent, beautiful story. My sisters and I were raised in those days where holidays were mostly spent at home doing almost nothing. Many times, we would gather in my mom's room exploring whatever we found exciting enough. From magazines to pictures and even our medical records.

However, year in year out, we were most intrigued by her collection of pictures. She had several moments of her growing up caught on camera. Same thing with my dad. Many milestones of our growing up were not left out too. I would spend time with my siblings feasting my eyes on the pictures all day long during the holidays.

While I was impressed about many of these memories, the pictures from their wedding ceremony stood out. Every important detail was captured: the traditional ceremony, holy matrimony, reception, and others. We all tried to identify the few people we knew in these pictures and would talk about the attire, cake, food, and many other details.

Strangely, I loved the world in the pictures more than our reality. Things were beginning to transition from all the love I knew to an unusual silence. Staring at the picture, there seemed to be loads of peace, love, and joy in there.

Life outside the picture was too simple, nothing exciting. Mom went to work regularly, and dad had not been around for some time. He worked outside our state and would come around on some weekends, but that had not been happening for a while.

As a child, there were no signs to warn about what was coming. I had a very peaceful upbringing. Besides the noise we made as kids and happy fun moments, there was no cause for alarm. I didn't witness any intense moment, not a fight or heated exchange of words. My friend had told me her parents would argue loudly and curse at each other, but that never happened in my home.

All through my growing years, my dad's job as a bank manager demanded that he worked outside our city and state. The once-in-a-while presence was becoming more obvious. My 8-year-old self was probably starting to notice it now. He was usually home one weekend a month, maybe a little more or less.

I guess that as any other child would, I wanted him more. The first time I realized this was during my sister's 10th birthday. I had been looking forward to this party. We had attended a couple of our friends' parties and I couldn't wait to have our own. There were lots of friends, balloons, cakes, and all the fun things.

As the party was ending, my dad arrived. He peeped into the venue with his regular clothes on. As his face disappeared, I assumed that he had gone to refresh from his long journey, get some party clothes on, and would be back to dive in. That never happened. That was one time I wanted more from him, not knowing what was to come.

On one of the weekends he was home, he sat with my sisters and me in our living room and spent some time with us. It felt a little unusual to have him pay that much attention to us. To cap the unusual attention and conversation, he told us he loved us so much. That was his first verbal expression of his love and it felt nice to hear that.

This one conversation was the last I had with him in our home as a child. That became the tipping point. Afterward, a long silent absence began, and that absence went on longer than I could ever imagine.

Unlike these days of access to communication, I only had to wait and hope something changed. Unfortunately, years rolled in, and change refused to show up.

For many young people, it wasn't a silent, prolonged absence like I experienced, it was a lot of messiness, negative emotions, and tension. Many witnessed things falling apart, they saw fights, third-party interferences, verbal or even physical abuse. They watched their parents argue and tear each other apart physically, even as their marriage was going down.

On the other hand, a good number of young people have no issues with physical presence. We had both parents, but possibly due to their poor lifestyle and choices, we were still unable to experience the love we desired from them. Some parents were distant, cold, uncaring, or even so problematic that we may even wish they were away.

If wishes were horses, everyone would love to grow in the best of environment with loving parents and endless resources. For many of us, life quickly bursts our bubbles and fails to deliver our wishes. As I experienced, different circumstances such as deaths, divorces, separations, absences, and birth by an unmarried mother feed us the unpleasant pill of growing up in the absence of one or both parents.

We do not choose to experience life this way and would change it if we could, but it becomes our reality, and we have to live through it. We see many others sheltered in their homes with an overdose of love and care. On the other hand, some of us get our first dose of dissatisfaction, rejection, pain, and hurt from our homes—the very first place that should have been our shelter.

I have had a few close people ask me, "Do you know what happened with your parents?" I don't and frankly, I don't think knowing would make me feel any better. Some know, others don't. Even those who know may never understand or make much sense of it. To a growing child, no excuse justifies being replaced by another, rejected, or abandoned.

For a long time, it was believed that parental separation had no impact on children, or that children were very resilient and would bounce back easily. However, years of research have proven that isn't entirely true.

Judith Wallerstein, a psychologist, and researcher monitored the lives of 100 children from divorced homes for 25 years, from childhood into adulthood. Her findings acknowledge that adults raised in divorced families carry within them a different kind of history. She discovered that as these children matured into adults, the pain of their parents' divorce was still affecting their relationships, their work, and their parenting.

My thoughts also echo that of the psychologist who believes there are no intelligent divorces or separation(s). Because the love between two people reflects on the people that matter to them, the departure of such love is always felt in the lives of those people.

WHOSE SIDE, MOM'S OR DAD'S?

Just around the season when my dad's absence was becoming more glaring, I was transitioning from primary to secondary school. Out of nowhere, I was told I would be going for a common entrance with my dad in the state he worked. I was super excited.
In my excitement, I didn't really give a thought to what that meant. If I was accepted to the school, I would have to move with my dad. I didn't consider that I would be leaving my mom, siblings, friends, and all I had known to a new place.

I had weeks to spend with my dad—It was the holiday season. I had never traveled, visited, or spent time with my dad. So, you can imagine I was filled with so much excitement that I was deaf to any other voice of reason. Before I knew it, we started the journey. I had never traveled that far and was drained at the end of that journey. Still, I looked forward to an amazing time.

It was a long journey and we had started late. My dad bought me some snacks and the trip started fine. The gap between us first became obvious when I couldn't tell my dad I needed to use the bathroom. It didn't help that Nigerian travel didn't give much room for convenience. I couldn't bring myself to tell my dad what was going on. I kept hoping we arrived at our destination. After what seemed like an eternity, we arrived!

My dad had set up private tutorials for me to prepare for the exam, so I was busy with that in the first week. Every day, I would stay with the tutor during the day and I was more focused on acing the exam. I wrote the exam and it was finally time to relax and enjoy.

My excitement was cut short as I would wake up every day to my dad's absence. He worked in a bank and lived on an extremely busy schedule. I would sometimes hear him dressing up for work in the mornings, but I was too sleepy to get up. During the nights, I tried to stay awake till he returned, but that wasn't successful either.

I spent my day with my aunt and older cousins. Not only were my cousins much older than I was, but they also would not spend time with me. There were also questions about my mom and siblings. It felt more like an interview. Besides, they could only ask. I could not talk about my family freely because I was afraid they were on the lookout for something wrong. I think the worst part was the chores from them.

Compared to what I had to do at home, I felt the chores were a truckload for someone my age. On a few lucky days, I got to visit my tutor and was happy to be away from them. I also preferred to spend more time with my aunt's neighbor than in my aunt's house.

Needless to say, I missed home dearly. I missed my three sisters; They always proved to be great company. Our holidays were spent together. We were so similar in all we did that every of my activity revolved around them. I was so happy to jump on board with my dad that I didn't take time to talk to them or consider them.

We never discussed our parents or whatever was going on. Possibly because we didn't witness negative events worth discussing or possibly because we were just content with what we had come to know. I just wanted to be with them and was no longer interested in this plan that would keep me torn apart from them.

In her book, *Between Two Worlds,* Elizabeth Marquardt touched on how parental separation burden children with the impossible task of trying to balance both sides. Her book which was from research that studied the lives of children of divorce for 20 years reflected how kids are left in the chaos, wondering how to intelligently hold it together with both sides of their homes, not wanting to offend either their dad or mom.

Making everyday decisions can easily become a nightmare. The loyalty conflict that comes with where to spend Christmas, who attends graduation parties, what to say or not say, where to draw the lines between confiding and divulging important information, or who gets to hear some news first are a few of the regular emotional turmoil they have to deal with.

Finally, the holiday with dad was over and it was time for me to return home. The result from my common entrance was not released yet and I was not bothered. I had been counting down to the day I would return home anyway. I returned home and that was the last I heard about the entrance exam or studying close to my dad. I'm not sure I was in any way interested at this point.

So, I went on to secondary school at the home I've always known, among the friends familiar to me and I settled fine. After this entire event, there was even more silence, more absence. Life continued with my mom and siblings. I cannot remember being told dad wasn't coming back, but I guess our young minds figured it out after a while. The memories of his sweet conversation with myself and my siblings lingered in my mind, but I couldn't find the one who said them.

Marital union is more than the two people primarily involved; more people, especially the children, are intimately connected. Its separation impacts every person that knows that union, from relatives to children's peers, to coworkers. When a couple decides to go solo, is there ever a perfect way their loved ones can keep a good side with both?

CHAPTER TWO

MAMA OVERDO

ALL FORGOTTEN

Absence always makes the heart fonder, they say. But not for this daddy's girl. That sentence never existed in my diary. I wasn't sure if it was because I didn't have my dad around all the time and I was used to a life with my mom before he left. Things just remained as usual. A lot of things had happened. So many milestones were reached, and it was all mama and her girls.

Days rolled by; the months passed in a flash, and the years came quickly. It had been over ten years of absence and I was in the university. In my second year in the university after taking a test, I found myself wondering if I had indicated the right information on my test sheet. Nothing is more worrisome for a student than not being sure you had attempted your exam questions correctly. It becomes worse if you remember a mistake vividly.

Not wanting to let my efforts slide, I decided to talk to the Professor in charge. It could not get any worse, the worst response would be a 'no' from the Professor, I concluded. As I sat in her office and mumbled incoherent words to explain my plight, she warmly and jokingly asked me what I had in mind as I wrote the test. She confirmed that I had all the right details which made me feel better.

As I turned to leave, she asked me, "Where are your parents?" I told her that I lived with my mom. Then she asked about my dad and I went silent. I was only in her office to talk about my test and I was not prepared for that question.

Not knowing what to tell her, there were a few moments of awkward silence. Finally, I made it to three words: *"He's no longer…"* Her words jolted me from my lost state. I was still gathering my thoughts to complete my sentence when she started apologizing. She told me she was sorry about my dad and for the upsetting question.

Apparently, she had concluded my dad was no longer alive. I guess because no one had asked me about him in a long time, I was lost. It was too late, and I was too frozen to tell her it was untrue. She said some warm words and assured me her office was open if I ever needed to talk to anyone. I walked out slowly dragging my feet as I considered changing the narrative; but no, it was just not possible at that moment.

As I stepped outside her office and walked to my hostel, I realized how much I had forgotten about my dad. There was no longer any space for him in my mind or life. Not only was he not missed, but he was also totally forgotten. Life with my mom and siblings was the life I had now. That life had so much peace, love, and joy. I was so content. I remembered the last time I had seen him. Our pastor had insisted on talking to him about his long absence. And as his beloved daughter, they took me along with them. It was a weekday and I had to miss school, but I was also happy I would be seeing him.

After the long journey, we arrived at his house. He was not at home, so we headed for the bank where he worked. I saw him far away walking quickly across the room, the next thing I was told was that it was time to go home. My heart sank. He barely talked to them and the trip was futile. I can't remember seeing him on that day.

I left with a bigger hole in my heart and an envelope that could barely resolve the mounting needs that were at home. I guess this event was the limit for me. I stopped caring anymore. Besides what was going on with my home, a lot was going on in the society I lived in.

My friend's parents were on the verge of a divorce and it wasn't the most pleasant thing as she had to sit and listen to both sides. I witnessed one of her conversations with her dad as he tried to explain the situation to his daughter, defending himself and faulting her mom. I could see the defeat in my friend's face, she was done listening to both sides and would rather be left alone.

There were so many ugly stories flying around. Husbands abandoning their homes to be with their mistresses; some at home as though they were absent. There were also stories of women tearing down their homes. My growing brain wanted peace and stability. I was content with all I had. We were one strong unit. So, little wonder dad was completely off my mind.

A MOTHER'S LOVE

"There is nothing as powerful as mother's love, and nothing as healing as a child's soul." - Unknown

A mom is a whole vibe! A single mom, even more. My mom isn't left out. She was an entire mix: teacher, caregiver, prayer warrior, driver, chef, referee, money bank, and even mosquito hunter. Yes! mosquito hunter. Growing up in the humid weather in Nigeria meant there were lots of mosquitoes around and as kids, we were never diligent enough to keep all the doors locked.

Every night, my mom would spend hours in our room praying for each one of us with the blue glass lantern while tracking mosquitoes flying around, until she decided we were old enough! If anything was hoping to prey on innocent us, my mom would approach it just as she did to the mosquitoes, fiercely and without apologies.

If anything was termed as the best, my mom wanted it for us. So, we went to the best catholic school in town. She would prepare us very early before the town was awake. Then, she would join us in catching the early morning bus before heading back home to prepare for her day.

We would always come home to lunch; until we started making silly choices for what we wanted.
She always had something she just learned to help us move forward. There was a time we had to eat an egg every day and no matter what we had for breakfast, there was always an extra egg for the day. There were days of *'Sunday-Sunday tablets',* a grueling ritual of having to take prophylaxis drugs for malaria every Sunday night.

She always went the extra mile. When we needed a book, she showed up with two. We would have to specifically give instructions that we needed only one, especially if it would result in waste.

During one of the festive seasons, she took apart her wedding gown to make beautiful designs on our pink dresses for us without our knowledge. Because I was obsessed with her wedding dress, I knew immediately where the beautiful designs came from. I was happy and sad at the same time; I loved my dress, but I also lost one of the wonders I loved to peek at in her room.

Her discipline was top-notch. She meted out good punishment when necessary and of course, I never wanted that, even when it was well deserved. I guess for her, raising us single-handedly was enough of a cross to bear. She wasn't ready to add a pile of our misbehavior to that; society was expecting too much from her!

The most important value I got from my mom was her life as a Christian. She was diligent with other things but extra diligent with her faith. Beyond praying over us as we slept, there were nights she kept us awake usually for about one hour to pray. Our family was not one to miss church. She signed us up for many camp meetings, seminars, and the likes.

Beyond living out her Christian life as an example, she set us on a path of excellence and leadership. Not once did she make an excuse out of the absence of our dad nor play the blame game. We heard no ill about him from her. Instead, she taught us what the values of sacrifice, hard work, and love were.

My uncle called my attention to her leadership early on, "Do you know when it comes to showing up, your mom is either at the frontline or not present at all?"

As I tried letting the weight of those words sink in, he quickly reminded me of how she led the association of secretaries in her university and spurred her colleagues into doing more in their careers. He moved on to the leadership roles she served in the church.

I was convinced without a doubt. At work, in our community, and church, mom was either in or out. Whenever she was involved in a group or community, she always put in her best. She was a natural leader and bore her responsibilities with so much grace. Her entrepreneurial skills were top-notch. As long as it could fetch clean money, she was in for it. She always had some side gig running with her work.

Just as she was committed to our lives, she showed commitment to others around her too. Especially those around her who would gladly use the little help she had to give. I was all set to face life. My home seemed like an ideal home.

I moved on as every other happy child because the love, peace, and strength I needed were available for me, right at home. I can hardly recount incidents where I felt down, was put down, or wished I had my dad present. All I had known in my life was my mom.

I wanted more for us as a family, more money, nice clothes, a beautiful house, and opportunities for beautiful vacations. But even all of that was just in the context of my mom and siblings. As the years passed by, I never for one day asked for or desired to have my dad. I was that child that fitted into the construct of the power of one strong adult.

According to this report, no matter the source of hardship, the single most common factor for children who end up doing well is having the support of at least one stable and committed relationship with a parent, caregiver, or any other adult.

Over the years, I have continued to take a deeper look at this construct. Truly, instability is a recipe for a tumultuous journey in a child's life. A stable home many times equals a successful child. Over the years, that definition of stability has changed in different ways. What was known as unstable some years ago may be the norm now and vice versa. That leaves me wondering who and what determines these rules?

Family structure has been dynamic throughout human history and across various societies. Growing up, polygamy was the big word. My friends experienced it. The media displayed it quite frequently. Husband-sharing was an ugly business, the pictures painted were all negative. Children growing up to realize their dads had other families; children learning fast to be loyal to their mothers among other women in their big household.

In modern times, single-parent households, cohabitation, same-sex families, and voluntary childless couples are increasingly common. Of all these types, recent trends tilt increasingly towards the single-parent household. More and more children are being raised by single parents, especially by moms.

Women are making these choices that are becoming commonplace. *Baby mamas* are the trend now. Women are readily relinquishing marital commitments to focus on raising children. DIY (Do It Yourself) moms who are older single women willing to commit to raising children on their own are boldly taking up the task, even through donor inseminations.

Well, society is in a good shape, you may say. To support these thoughts, research has shown that belonging to a single-mother household builds resilience in some children and sets them into living independently early in life. The question is, can that be ascertained from a good number of such cases?

Parental separation has continued to receive an overhaul to ensure it ends well for all those involved. That's why we have services such as *'Intelligent Divorce'*. Programs like this are in place today to approach parental separation properly, and ensure that the impact on families, especially on the kids, is reduced. It sounds like things are not so bad right?

Another support for single homes comes from an understanding also backed by research that children were emotionally better off if they were raised by a single mother rather than if they stayed in a home with two warring married parents. Notice that the benchmark of this comparison is having one or two bad parents.

When asked about the sensitive issue of divorce in His time, Christ's explanation was very clear. "*He saith unto them, Moses because of the hardness of your hearts suffered you to put away your wives: but from the beginning it was not* so" (Matt. 19:8 KJV).

Although this was the situation over 2,000 years ago, it doesn't look too different even in our time. We are now in the 21st century, and it's been 6,000 years since God created man. It seems God's original plan is now thousands of years obsolete. Or possibly, God's people no longer understand what it means. Or maybe it has just become so natural to assimilate the current trend around us?

Well, His plan is well-detailed in His word, *"Did he not make them one, with a portion of the Spirit in their union? And what was the one God seeking? Godly offspring."* (Malachi 2:15)

The union of a man and woman is God's perfect atmosphere for raising His offspring. God is so interested that He gave out specific instructions for orphans and the fatherless in verses of the scripture.

With the decay in the marital institution, how can the marital union still be God's ideal scenario for every child? What do we say about the death of a parent(s) or marriages where lives are at risk? No matter what the scenario may be in the society we now live in or what norm is now prevalent, one thing is certain; God didn't want it this way, it wasn't so in the beginning!

CHAPTER THREE

SEEMING DISADVANTAGE

ANYTHING MISSING?

It was a beautiful day and out of the hustle and bustle of my laboratory routine, I got a little bit of free time and I was spending some of it on social media. My friend was celebrating her dad's birthday and had put up a post on social media reliving the wonderful moments she shared with her amazing father while growing up.

She mentioned how she had gotten lots of profound insights, life lessons, and enjoyed memorable moments with her dad. Not just her, but herself and her siblings.

From cooking and feeding them, to being involved in their academics and guiding them through difficult life decisions including career and marriage; she left no stone unturned.

That was a picture I didn't see on my end. Her friends who had shared some of those moments lined up to paint a better picture than she had done. I looked through the conversation, there was no way I could fit in with my dad in any of the scenarios she had painted. Does that sound similar?

That same week, I had heard two mentors talk about how much confidence their fathers built into them to face the world. Their dads were their cheerleaders as they journeyed through life. These fathers had taken their time to teach their kids life lessons that can rarely be found within the walls of the classroom and had set them moving on their roads to success.
A relationship coach I respect so much also shared how much freedom she had discussing relationships with men with her father. She learned firsthand about men and other life relationships from her dad.

Of all these testimonies, that of my friend's dad hit differently. Perhaps reading such an experience from someone with whom I navigated childhood drove the point home clearly and painfully.

I began to think. Yes, we were all kids and while growing up, each of our circumstances seemed to be the same. We went to the same high school and college, had similar church experiences, and grew up in about the same neighborhood. But, I didn't have one thing that she enjoyed— a father's love.

By the time I was through with my social media time, not only did I get the distraction I needed for some minutes, I was left feeling disadvantaged and with a huge load of resentment against my background for not providing me the opportunities my friend enjoyed.

Before these events, I had never considered how weighty and important the role of a father is in the life of a child. I had no doubts my life was all great, but that week I started to realize it could have been even greater. I recounted loads of opportunities I had missed all because I wasn't confident enough.

Although I never did badly in school, I stayed away from anything outside class because I never thought I was good enough. If anything was competitive, the best way I dealt with it was to walk away. I imagined if I had a dad like my mentor's dad who always encouraged and spoke the right words to me, I could have made better decisions.

Thankfully, this feeling did not last long enough to ruin the rest of my day or life. It didn't leave me the same way either. It brought me to a time of deep reflection over what I had missed growing up. I had been blind to the blessings of a father's presence over a child's life. A part of me had come to see my circumstances as the norm.

Single parenting bore a lot of stigma decades back when it wasn't this common. In recent times, with an increasing number of families being headed by one parent, I'm thankful that I didn't have to deal with very obvious stigma as a child. I gladly accepted the norm it had become. I am not sure if the latter was any helpful in shaping my perspective of fatherhood.

I felt like I was robbed of a good part of my childhood; an entire world was hidden from me. I sought to know what masked this knowledge. I wondered why I also didn't pay attention to the vacuum until much later. Was it because life had always been with my mom? Probably because no one talked about it or modeled it.

Or maybe it had become a norm and I just didn't know life could be different?

THE "*LAS LAS*" AFFIRMATION

There is a common phrase in the Nigerian society today. As good as it sounds, when it comes to certain obvious issues, it irks me so badly. For a lack of a better word, I call it the *Las Las Affirmation*. Simply put, *Las Las* means after all we've been through, we came out fine. It is commonly used in present situations too and you commonly hear *"Las las, everything will be fine"*

Being fine shouldn't only be something we fight or strive to have, it is an advantage we have as God's children. Remember the prayers of our fathers of faith, *Beloved, I pray that in every way you may prosper and enjoy good health, as your soul also prospers* – 3 John 1:2.

The *las las* phrase commonly speaks to the resilience and optimistic spirit of Nigerians, being fine despite the odds. On the flip side, it has become a phrase that is commonly used to ignore sensitive significant issues, a cliché especially in the context of a difficult upbringing.

Over and over again as people share their difficult past, they quickly mop it all up with the *Las Las Affirmation*.

For a long time, I belonged to the *las las* camp. I affirmed over and over that regardless of my background I turned out perfectly. So, when I hear such phrases, I understand where they are coming from. *I have passed through a fire, but I don't smell of smoke*. Well, we are not one of the 3 men in the furnace with biblical Daniel. We might have been bruised but not crushed! So, what about the bruises?

In her book, *Childhood Disrupted: How Your Biography Becomes Your Biology, and How You Can Heal,* Donna Jackson Nakazawa masterfully highlights the complexity of how early life adversity imprints on our biology and stalks our health and wellbeing into our adult lives.

She captured it succinctly by saying *"Parental love is a boon for life. Feeling loved and seen for who we are, and supported to become who we hope to become, pays forward mentally and physically throughout our lives."* What happens to those who didn't get that?

Yes, the past is past for a reason, but is it really in the past? What many call the past may no longer be their present reality, but may remain an ever-present negative influence over their lives. The past spills into the present and a tough childhood can translate into a tumultuous, challenging adulthood.

Digging up and dealing with the past is something we don't want to dwell on. We are eager for what lies ahead, trusting that we are on the path towards a brighter tomorrow. However, we can only move away from past events when they are processed as experiences to learn from and grow. We have a choice to either deal with it or look away.

Left undealt with, past challenges keep us hooked into the emotional charge of the time. So, before we ride on the waves of the *las las* talk, we must take an inventory of the state of our hearts if we don't want to live in deception carved out by our hearts. Because...*the human heart is the most deceitful of all things* - Jeremiah 17:9

The heart of the matter is the matter of the heart.

CHAPTER FOUR

MATTERS OF THE HEART

As I continued down the week of my amazing fatherhood discovery, an intriguing conversation I had with an older friend came to my mind. She had shared with me how her seemingly healthy cousin had to go through surgery due to a heart condition. Unknown to this cousin and everyone else, he had lived with this condition all his life. Although he had a tugging concern about his health, he couldn't pin it on anything. All he knew was that he got tired easily. This had gone on for years; neglected but ever-present.

Although he was able to go about his daily routine, he couldn't do more. When he decided that he had had enough of the weird feeling in his body, he finally sought medical help. When the results of his tests came out, he realized that he had suffered from a heart condition for a very long time, possibly since birth.

Although he could go on with life living with all the symptoms he had always had, he also had the choice of being operated upon. Wanting to do more with his life and experience even more strength, he chose to have the surgery done.

As I laid in my bed reflecting over my recent concerns about my upbringing, I began to feel like that cousin. My heart didn't feel sick physically, but I felt there was a discomfort right within my soul that had suddenly sprung up to the surface and caught me by surprise.

While it looked unrelated, I dug the internet for more information on such heart diseases. I realized it was possible to live with heart conditions; sometimes with symptoms that can easily be neglected.

Many times, such conditions are only picked up when such persons get frustrated by their symptoms and decide to get checked. Other times, the truth unfolds when new demands are placed on the heart. A new activity as basic as running or starting a new job could begin to exert greater demands on the heart, revealing its true weak state. I felt like the true state of my heart had just been revealed after running a marathon on the tracks of life with my friend.

A human heart is approximately the size of a large fist, yet it is essential to our survival. When the heart starts failing or stops functioning, the human body would quickly cease to function properly. Little wonder there are many ideas in the world today to help us preserve our hearts from hurt and easily pick up signals when our hearts start to fail.

Just like our physical hearts, our 'emotional hearts' are also very central to our functioning. It is the source of everything else in our life: overflowing into thoughts, words, and actions. In the words of the popular author, Michael Hyatt, "If our heart is unhealthy, it threatens everything else—family, friends, career—everything!"

Ask many people raised by a single parent, it is just one of the things one has to live with. There is an increasing proportion of the world's children being raised by a single parent, especially mothers. Taking a moment to reflect on the state of our hearts is one thing no one talks about. Everyone just wants to move on. Many times, we would rather talk about how well we have fared, until reality hits!

Truly, as children from non-traditional homes, our outcomes are as varied as possible. The impact of our homes is usually not the same for everyone; it differs hugely. Not only is the difference seen from home to home, but it is also commonly seen among siblings in the same household.

Some individuals feel very burdened about the state of their homes and how it impacts their lives. Some suppress these feelings in every way possible and would rather not think or talk about them. Others feel less negatively impacted by their background and would not be bothered about this topic.

It is well acknowledged that many children from non-traditional families have the same success as those with married parents. Many times, we usually believe and make others believe we are doing just fine. Our upbringing is believed to teach us resilience, responsibility, and independence very early in life.

When we think about others going through the same experience, we believe we are doing fine. We are not a mess. We are not dealing with any serious mental health issues, neither are we trading our bodies for money nor looting the society. Many of us are calm, thriving, decent people building a successful life. A good job we are doing with our lives or so it seems.

However, in our closets, some become confronted with the realities and peculiarities of our lives. Many of us bear deep-seated issues. A deep and sincere reflection of our lives would usually reveal beliefs, fears, mindsets, and attitudes that stem the experiences in our homes.

Many times, our comportment and successes are simply our masks, hiding away our hurts, fears, distrust, and vulnerabilities.
Beneath the strong successful persona is that small child seeking explanations, yearning for love, trust, peace, help, and strength. So, what good will going to the past do? Reflecting over hurts is not to keep us hurt for the rest of our lives. Just like my friend's cousin, it helps us make a wise choice for healing, relieves us of many baggage we've unknowingly carried around for years while protecting us from future breakdown.

HOW HAVE WE FARED?

'No wonder', 'I see'...

What are your thoughts when you realized someone behaving wrongly is being raised or was raised in a non-traditional family? We have all been conditioned to believe that growing in such situations is a disadvantage. Knowing the strain that the absence of one or both parents put on a child's life, I have caught myself replying with any of the words above. I am not alone. We begin to ask in such situations, where is his/her mother or father? We quickly trace the roots of the problem to their upbringing. Why is this the case? Do we truly know that these seeming disadvantages truly exist?

The truth is that *the stats do not lie*. Over the years, we have become witnesses of the impact of unstable and unhealthy family backgrounds on a child's development. While we have sketchy experiences that give us some idea and paint an overall picture, studies over several decades provide reliable information that points to the fact that inadequacies and deficits in family units and upbringing increases the risk of poor outcomes in children from such families.

A brief look into the statistics paints a reliable and more accurate picture of the burden of this problem. First, how many young people have to deal with growth in the absence of one or both parents? Studies have shown that all over the world, the number of children under single parents has continued to grow.

In Africa, single-mother families have continued to grow because of out-of-wedlock motherhood, marital instability, and widowhood[1]
In Nigeria, as far back as 2006, millions of women-led their homes; close to 3 million women-led their homes due to divorce, separation, or the deaths of their husbands.[2]

The numbers are even much higher in other developed regions of the world. In Britain and the US for example, almost one out of every four homes with kids are headed by single parents.[3]

---

[1] Health effects of single motherhood on children in sub-Saharan Africa: a cross-sectional study Lorretta FC Ntoimo & Clifford O Odimegwu BMC Public Health volume 14, Article number: 1145 (2014)

[2] Commission NP: Population Census of the Federal Republic of Nigeria. 2006, Abuja: National Population Commission, 2009

[3] https://www.pewresearch.org/fact-tank/2019/12/12/u-s-children-more-likely-than-children-in-other-countries-to-live-with-just-one-parent/

The next question is, does it truly matter? Beyond speculations that we may share, several studies tell the story of how the absence of parents influences kids' behavior and successes.

A compelling example of such stories is Judith Wallerstein's 25-year study of one hundred children of divorce. Judith followed up and interviewed these children at 18 months and then 5, 10, 15, and 25 years after the divorce to find out how they fared.

Judith's study showed disheartening results. Even twenty-five years after the divorce, these children continued to experience substantial expectations of failure, fear of loss, fear of change, and fear of conflict.

On a broader outlook, it is well acknowledged that children of divorced parents are more likely to have poor academic performance, increased risk of destructive behaviors, poorer health, marital instability. Living with single parents means having a higher likelihood of being poor, committing crimes, or using drugs[4]. Fathers' absence has a profound impact on

---

4 https://diarysheets.wordpress.com/2012/01/23/adam-mitchells-speech-for-fathers-courageous/

educational attainment, children's social-emotional health, and adult mental health.[5]

Is it all gloomy for young people growing up this way? The short answer is No. It is not all negative. Other studies have shown that certain positive traits are developed even in these circumstances.
Some say that when it comes to life satisfaction, quality of their peer relationships, or positivity about family life, children who grow in unfavorable family backgrounds have similar or even higher rate as their peers.

Not all children raised in disadvantaged backgrounds suffer these adverse outcomes, are doomed, or have lives riddled with problems, poverty, and misery. What these statistics show is that the risks of poor outcomes are greater for them.

Do you see yourself in these scary statistics? It's very likely, you don't. But, what about many other little things these statistics do not commonly uncover? Things like maybe we are lucky enough not to find

---

5 The Fatherhood Principle: God's Design and Destiny for Every Man by Myles Munroe

ourselves in the camp of people suffering from these increased risks. The truth still stands. Our experiences growing up in our homes always leave an indelible mark in our lives even as we transition into adults and away from our homes.

A COMMON THEME

The stats show the figures, the world recognizes a common theme.

I didn't understand my professor's questions about my family until I started working as an undergraduate lecturer. In one of my few years in the university, I had to guide students through the process of registering for their classes at the start of the semester. One of the students in that class had a few questions she wanted to ask me.

As she walked in, the fear and worries in her heart could not be hidden. She wanted to know why she was not permitted to proceed on the industrial attachment program like many of her friends. She had failed several classes and needed to repeat them before she could be allowed to proceed on to the program.

As I went on explaining to her, she seemed to have had enough with life. Obviously, the school situation was adding more to her overwhelming problems. The look of discouragement and pain moved me to ask a couple of questions that have always come up whenever students were in a difficult situation.

I came to find out that she had lost her dad the past year and needed to start living with an uncle. It didn't look like she was in a good place in life and she was fed up. Unfortunately, a couple of months later, she stopped showing up in school and never returned. Sadly, this was not the first or the last of such incidences I experienced.

Very early on in my job, I observed that one of the first questions students going through difficult times were asked had to do with the state of their homes. Everyone was aware of the impact that challenges in the families had on children from such families, even as young adults.

The school system is designed to test one thing - a student's academic performance. However, academic performance is a product of many factors. When a student is tested, emotional and mental well-being are also being tested and the home plays a huge role here.

Academics is just one of the facets of life that test more than an individual's capabilities.

Every phase of our lives indirectly tests the quality of our homes. We are all tested, and the home tells the results we produce. When self-worth, compassion, confidence, vulnerability, and so many other life strengths are tested, our homes scream out loud in response.

If there's anything our society does so well, it is labeling. Our society is quick to see us through the lens of our experiences including what happens in our home. The children are not spared, neither is the single parent, especially if it's a woman. I guess that may explain the circle of friends that were closest to my mom - women in similar circumstances. It is funny how fathers are spared but not the mothers.

Being a single mother, especially if the man is still alive, is a sign of a failed woman in the African context. A failed marriage is the woman's fault, regardless of the circumstances leading to it. I have heard stories of single moms being perceived as potential husband snatchers by fellow women, or as a threat by insecure men, all because of their status.

For the children, the theme explains why we are thought to be 'broken', ill-raised, ignorant, aggressive and suffer emotionally and behaviorally. I guess you can agree with me over and over again that you and I have proved this stereotype wrong many times. Not everyone turns out so badly.

So, why do we still have these stereotypes? The truth is that these stereotypes persist because some people fell into these stereotypes in the past and some continue to fall into them even today.

CHAPTER FIVE

LIFE HURDLES

"You did very well in the entrance exam," lady A said. "Oh, really? That's exciting news" I thought to myself as I quickly excused myself from the adult conversation between my mom and Lady A. The conversation continued in my absence even as I dealt with the mixed emotions in my mind. Why is no one talking about me resuming in this new school?

After all, it was already a few weeks into the new school year, when will I get to join this new school? Why was mom acting indifferent? We have all been waiting for this good news. On the other hand, I felt happy. Finally, since there was now good news about this new school, my dream of reconnecting with the friends I made in the short time I visited the school may be coming true.

A few months before this time, Lady A had just told my mom about this amazing new school and I started to prepare for the application process. I wrote an entrance examination and attended a 3-day interview for admission to the new school some miles away from home.

I loved what I saw. I had never seen a school in such a serene and beautiful environment. I also made good friends in those 3 days. My mom was as elated as I was about the entire experience. It was a Christian school belonging to one of the big churches in Nigeria. I already started to imagine how the uniforms would look on me. I was going to have great friends too, so I wouldn't miss much. We all waited patiently for the results.

As I returned to the spot where my mom and her guest were discussing, I began to hear mom complain, "It is a great place indeed, but the cost is just too much." Lady A said the same thing too. She went on to tell my mom I was one of the top ten students from the interview, the fifth precisely. My heart fluttered when Lady A announced that I got some discount for being in the 5th position. "Well, even with the discount that she gets, the bill is just a lot," my mom responded.

Now, I understood why mom wasn't excited about the news; why she held the letter so loosely like it was just any sheet of paper. At that moment, I realized my dream had been crushed. I zoned out of all my dreams immediately. I just didn't have any reason to feel hurt. Knowing the situation in my home, I turned my frustration at the school. Why would they charge so much?

A quick flashback to earlier events in my current school jump-started me to the reality of my situation. "Wura, the principal is calling you", a student called out to me in a typical Nigerian student style.

There were only a few reasons the principal would need my attention, so I hurriedly left whatever I had going on and headed straight for the principal's office. As I got closer to the principal's office, I saw a few people that made me guess what the call was all about. Our school fees were yet to be paid! But why would they bother us again? I thought our parents had asked for an extension.

As soon as I joined the others, the principal asked those of us whose parents had requested a formal extension to return to class. It was almost 6 months into an industrial strike action at my mom's place of work with no payment of salaries. Because a good number of students in the school were affected by this, the parents had written to the school for an extension.

It sounded like a perfect excuse, at least, we had real reasons for defaulting. There were days when there were no excuses and we had been sent home, it was always an annoying experience because my friends never defaulted.
So, you can imagine why I deleted the new school from my heart. If this current one was way cheaper and we had such issues, it was better to drop the new school idea as soon as I could. I knew what my reality was and what was obtainable for me.

The new school kids all looked so good that I probably would stand out like a sore thumb. How will I tell them all the things happening back home? Well, maybe I was better off where I was. I quickly accepted my fate as other memories ran through my head. How will I explain the pap and plantain selling to these friends?

Yes! With all of our expenses falling on my mom, she needed extra sources of money. So, from making pap for domestic use, she started making pap for sale in our estate. At first, all we had to do was notify our mom when someone was at the door. Soon enough, we got initiated into the long laborious processing of the pap almost every week.

Then, mom decided to add plantain. Mom got a spot for us to sit right in front of the main street in our estate. We added our voice to convince her about the spot, but all that was on my mind was the opportunity to get out of the house and spend time with friends. And for the time it lasted, we did the same thing every evening; show up with fresh irresistible plantains.

My mom was the best at what she did and that reflected even in the quality of produce she got for resale. It was a lot of fun hanging out there in the evenings. It was on one of those evenings that I decided to spice up our fun by spinning around in circles. Everyone took their turns and when it was my turn, I lost control while spinning.

Everything became black. I stirred slowly as I heard my name being called. As I tried pulling myself together, sharp pains pierced through my head. Tasting blood in my mouth, I burst into tears as I recollected what had just happened. Somehow, we made the short trip home and of course, my mom had a million questions about my bruised swollen head, bloody mouth, and tears-soaked face. That was enough sign that our time on the street needed to end.

However, that didn't stop my mom's enterprising nature. Soon, she moved on to rent a small space which we took turns managing till I left college. There are many more events of my childhood; not having the best food or clothes, missing out on exciting adventures, and watching our friends have fun and not being able to join all because of money consequences.

Everyone has their fair share of difficult moments. But missing a whole chunk of one or both parents is different. Beyond the hurtful feelings we may be dealing with, we are also confronted by the sad reality that when it comes to building the life that we desire, we are at a disadvantage. Not only money issues, but time, commitment, affection among other things. It's often easy to wonder how life may have been better if we had both parents.

Vacations, camps, swimming, or piano lessons remain dreams because our single parents or guardians are struggling with their financial responsibilities or have other time commitments. When it comes to critical defining moments in our lives, we have no one to lean on or are limited to the support of one parent who might be too overwhelmed to see our struggles.

I quickly learned about the power of imagination. I spent many times rehearsing great moments from favorite TV series and novels and soon, I created my own scripts in my head; pictures of the beautiful life I would have when I grow up. Although I felt far from them in my present reality, I kept painting a beautiful picture of the future me every time I saw luxury cars, beautiful people, and gorgeous clothes. And that for me, was enough reason to stay hopeful.

THE DISADVANTAGED CONDITIONING

Just like any other student out of secondary or high school, I was both excited and anxious. I had written my JAMB (Joint Matriculation Examination Board) exam so that I could be considered for admission to a reputable university.

While I kept preparing and hoping to get admitted to some of my choice schools, mom came up with another idea. She wanted me to study outside my home country for my first degree. She was excited when two of her work colleagues were able to provide her with the right information on the admission process. Although she shared the news with positivity and excitement, I was far from excited.

The bottom line for me was money. Yes, money! "How much will it cost?" I asked her. Well, just talk to these 2 people and I will take it from there (referring me to her colleagues to get more information) I simply nodded my head. I knew I wasn't seeing them. All I thought about was how bad the idea was.

With my sister enrolled in a private university at that time, I couldn't see the possibility of that happening. Where would the money come from? All I felt was sympathy for my mom; doing that would put more financial stress on her. I wasn't ready to allow the ray of hope to shine in my mind at all. Besides, I refused to talk about it and didn't follow up with the process.

More important than what we are going through is what goes on within us. Simply put, our mind is that part of us that thinks, reasons, feels, understands, and remembers. Carolyn Dweck, the author of the best-selling book, *Mindset,* describes how negative labels work in the minds. Labels hamper achievements, hijack people's abilities and tell them where they belong. The news and stats around us, our own experiences tell us the same thing, that we are disadvantaged.

While all the information serves a different purpose—for instance, the stats help government and non-governmental organizations incorporate the right infrastructures—they speak differently to our minds. Bit by bit, they continue to pile up and become a stronghold in our minds.

As we acknowledge our disadvantages, we become disempowered in our minds and conditioned to certain patterns. We form a "self-perception" or "self-theory" about ourselves. Eventually, most people become a product of the information our minds and lives have been fed, whether good or bad, right or wrong. Our disadvantages begin to create in our minds the notion that certain things are not for us. These mindsets hold us back from living to our fullest potential. We give up on many battles without giving it a try at all.

Many times, except when we take an inventory of our lives, the effect of this conditioning usually goes unnoticed even when it continues to steer our lives down the path of disadvantage. And when we go through this route, the result is inevitable. We put limits on ourselves and clip our wings to fly within safe limits. Yes, there are a few exceptional stories of people who challenged these experiences and information, the number is very few.

Most people remain the product of the information their minds and lives have been fed, whether good or bad. All of our experiences stay with us, leaving imprints on our minds and becoming a part of us that we cannot be separated from. From my experience with not attending the school I loved because of costs, delayed school fees payment, and other financial struggles, I quickly learned to identify things that seem beyond me and not make an attempt for such things.

Our minds are fed by many sources. One important source that feeds our minds as children are the experiences from our home. Childhood events and memories can mysteriously work their way deep into our hearts and minds often subconsciously. Events such as parental divorce, separation, neglect, or death leave young minds with a barrage of negative feelings.

It is not uncommon to find ourselves believing we are unworthy of love— a mistake or a burden. These feelings seep into our subconscious minds, program our minds, and begin to determine how we navigate through life. These feelings usually become a foundation on which other external factors build on.

Sometimes, we hear a few exceptional stories of people who refuse to be held back by the unpleasant experiences that stem from their backgrounds. Many times, such people have to fight information that has seeped into their minds and reprogram their minds to positivity.

Without purging ourselves of our limiting and disadvantaged beliefs, we give up too easily. What we fail to realize is that we cannot win the battles that we make no attempts to try. When I hear the success stories of many today, I wonder if I could have gotten some scholarships that would have eased my financial constraints. But because I never gave it a trial or followed up with the right people, I closed the doors for such opportunities, my circumstances have no blame!

CHAPTER SIX

DAD IS DESTINY

Father's Day! What does Father's Day mean to you? Every year, people from all over the world set apart a day to appreciate an amazing figure and role model that is as ancient as man himself. And while it paints wonderful pictures of the amazing role a father plays in the life of a child; the scenario is not the same for every child.

Every Father's Day, I stare in awe of the wonderful things people have to say about their dads. How much does having a father mean? How does the presence of a father influence the trajectories of our lives? Especially in these times where there is a massive shift from what used to be to the norm to these times where fatherlessness continues to be on an increase.

On a particular Father's day several years ago, the words on a popular News Report bled from the newsstand into the hearts of many. Titled *Why Fathers Count*, the article affirmed: "Dad is destiny" Why Fathers? Why make such a bold statement on Father's day and not on Mother's Day? Mother's Day seems more pronounced and is even celebrated more than once in some places. Besides, both parents play an equally important role in the life of a child.

The statement was just not from perception or hearsays; it was backed up by statistics to drive home the point. Using stats on income, incarceration, substance use among others, the article went on to explain that "more than any other factor, a father's presence in the family determines a child's success and happiness."

More and more leaders have continued to lend their voices to the importance of the role of a father. World-renowned leader and author, Dr. Myles Munroe, in his book, *The Fatherhood principle* describes Dad's destiny as a statement that embodies both the problem and solution for the majority of our societies' ills.

In a speech promoting responsible fatherhood, titled, 'No Excuses', former US President, Barack Obama, said:

"Of all the rocks upon which we build our lives, we are reminded that family is the most important. And we are called to recognize and honor how critical every father is to that foundation. They are teachers and coaches. They are mentors and role models"

Testimonies from law-enforcement agents describe the deep hurt and devastation that fatherlessness produces in a child's life[6]. They describe prisons as places full of men and women who lived recklessly after being abandoned by their fathers. Some are wounded by the men who should have loved them the most. Many now follow the same pattern of irresponsibility that their fathers did.

Fatherlessness is an "elephant" in the room, a topic few leaders seem to be addressing or at least addressing proactively to facilitate change. Yet, society remains plagued by its effect. While many mothers have shouldered on and sacrificed to raise their children, they were neither designed nor equipped to bear it alone.

Are there motherless homes? Of course, there are! Does motherless count? Of course, it does! Two things make the subject of fatherlessness particularly noteworthy. When it comes to single-parent homes, the majority have fathers absent. When it comes to the gaps the absence of a parent creates, fatherlessness screams louder.

WHAT DO FATHERS DO?

The closest I saw about a father's role was from my friend's dad. Those roles were very defined and consistent. Every morning, her dad was responsible for dropping her off at school. Then, he took care of the money details, paying school fees and providing money to keep the house running. He was hardly at home except for the mornings and weekends.

Are fathers just supposed to be married to their work and be absentee landlords? Or just a "Sunday institution" in the home? As the proliferation of mother-headed families continues to increase and survive, would fathers' presence or absence matter anymore? After all, if fathering is no different from mothering, it makes perfect sense to carry on without them.

It seems like there are more finely defined details on how much a mom is needed: warmth, love, protection, nurturing, and many more. However, when it comes to the public discussion about fathering, it is seldom acknowledged that fathers have a distinctive role to play in the lives of their children. After all, if fathering is no different from mothering, males can easily be replaced in the home by women.

The things fathers do seem to have evolved as societies have evolved. As the lines on a father's role continue to blur, the truth about the importance of the marital union for the children still stands true as we see in Malachi 2:15. *God has made them one… And what was the one God seeking? Godly offspring.*

Is there anything like a dad privilege? I believe there is. The privileged ones around me have told a story of a very present father growing up. Their fathers took care of provision in all regards - roof, food, encouragement, among others. They also talked about expectations. Expectations to be the best, good students, good people. Not only did fathers expect the best from them, but they also provided the stimulation and set a pace for them to follow.

Is there anything like fixed roles for each parent to do? I don't think so. Much of what they contribute to the growth of their children, of course, is simply the result of being a second adult in the home. Bringing up children is demanding, stressful, and often exhausting.

Two adults cannot only support and help each other; they can also offset each other's deficiencies and leverage each other's strengths.

What fathers do, and don't do is directly evident in many of our most grievous social ills. While there are no fixed roles, some attributes stand out over and over again.

Fathers are important to their sons as role models. They are important for maintaining authority and discipline. And they are important in helping their sons develop both self-control and feelings of empathy toward others; character traits that are found to be lacking in violent youth.

Fathers are the first and most important men in the lives of young girls. They provide male role models, accustoming their daughters to male-female relationships. Engaged and responsive fathers play with their daughters and guide them into challenging activities. They protect them, providing them with a sense of physical and emotional security. Girls with adequate fathering are more able, as they grow older, to develop constructive heterosexual relationships based on trust and intimacy.

WHERE DO WE GO FROM HERE?

From disadvantaged beliefs, mindsets, and attitudes, to absent daddy privileges, how farther down the road of disadvantage will we allow our homes take us?
If a quarter of the world population has lived through childhood without all the love, affection, and support that comes from two loving parents, has it become the new normal? Is our society prepared to address all the disadvantages and deficits that may be present with our upbringing or do we just ignore them altogether?

Debate remains ongoing on how much the world has improved over the decades. When dropping mortality rates, child death, women empowerment, and technological developments are considered, many believe the world has improved.

However, can the same be said about the way our world views parenting and upbringing? Will our world ever strive to make the homes we are born into better? I have had to ask myself, will everyone be born into a world that provides all they need? Will there be a perfect growing experience for every young person? The answer to this is a very easy *No.*

If this is the case, then where do we go from here? How can we keep our lives free from the toxic debris of the environment we grew in or are growing in? How do we make up for the deficits and weaknesses that hold us back? Is there any hope for any individual that is caught up in the web of their background?

It is uncommon to find a home that does not provide a good measure of positive input in a child's life, no matter how small. However, the negatives easily swallow up the positives. It is not enough to only realize the extent of the negativity that we have been exposed to in our homes. Thriving even amid these negativities and triumphing over them is what helps us build the beautiful life we all desire.

CHAPTER SEVEN

COMING AFTER ME

DREAMS!

I woke up calmly. This time I was very alert. What just happened? I had my fair share of dreams as a young child. Nightmares sometimes, but I never told anyone about it. I guess this was because I would usually feel safe as it ended and wouldn't get up from my sleep most times. Somehow, I could remember very faintly what had happened when I woke up, but it didn't matter. Good or bad, I never thought of sharing it and kept it to myself.

After I became a little older, I stopped having such dreams, until one night. I was probably about 12 years old when I had this very simple but thought-provoking dream. Although I didn't understand it, I knew it was different from what I had experienced over the years.

As much as I try not to sound unnecessarily spooky or spiritual, this one-sentence dream remains a reference point for my journey. In my dream, I had no idea where I was or what I was up to. All I knew was that I was standing in pitch darkness. And then, I heard a rather strange voice from a distance: *Where are you?* It was first about the voice. It sounded quite mystical, out of this world. Then, I turned immediately to the direction of the voice and all I saw was a light, very bright light, nothing else. That was all I saw.

Even though I haven't dreamt in years, this felt a little different. I could almost hear the voice reverberating and echoing in my ears. *"What was that?"* I asked, but there was no one to answer my question. Although I shared a room with my sister, she was sound asleep as it was midnight already. After tossing around for a while, I fell asleep. The next morning, I had completely forgotten my experience.

Later that day, as I spent my afternoon with my friend, I remembered and shared with her. We talked about every ridiculous thing: siblings, parents, classmates, teachers, and of course, boys. As I narrated my dream to her, she didn't show any expression.

Knowing how much energy we shared, the conversation wasn't going in the direction I wanted. She was either not interested in the subject or I was not making any sense. Either way, I figured out the best thing to do was to drop the conversation.

As I thought about her reaction afterward, I felt so stupid. Maybe it didn't really matter. If my very good friend who I told everything to didn't make sense of this, then who would? So, I never discussed it again with anyone else, not my siblings, mom, or other friends at church or school.

Years down the road, I realized I wasn't wrong after all. My experience was simply history repeating itself; not from fifty or a hundred years, but straight from the very first book of the bible. The book of Genesis is probably the most read book of the bible. If we have spent any time going through Genesis, then we are familiar with a sad yet hopeful account of man's fall out with God and a glimpse into God's heart reaching out for the lost.

"WHERE ARE YOU?"

A few years after my dream, I was listening to a sermon in church and as the Pastor preached, the words jumped back at me, *"Where are you?"* I could feel the tingling sensations in my ears, the echoes from that dream from my childhood; an eerie feeling of déjà vu settled over me.

I tried shaking it off, but it stayed with me all day. It sounded so familiar that I had to settle down to reflect and recollect the dream. I still remember. Then, I began to ask; could it be the same thing? What was this question all about?

Once again, I knew I needed to figure out if my dream meant anything. At this point, I still could not ask anyone. So, I turned to the bible for answers. As I spent more time reading the bible, I realized that for every man who had a relationship with God, there was a pattern of interruptions. A moment where bible characters were sought out by God.

Not all were dreams, there were diverse forms of ways through which God sought His people. From very simple daily life experiences to encounters by God Himself.

So, I started to ask, was this God seeking for His own? I also realized that this was the very first question that God asked the first man. Adam had flouted God's instructions and went into hiding when He heard God coming into the garden. I imagined Adam hearing God from afar but hiding away out of sight. And God asked him, "Where are you?"

"So, God asks us questions", I thought in my head. And this particular question came up because there was a drift in man's relationship with God.
There were no such questions before then. That question felt more like a call to order to a lost soul. And that bright light, and I standing in darkness didn't just sit right with me. I asked myself all the questions that flooded my heart. Desiring to right my wrongs as soon as I could.

As much as I asked my questions and desired to right my wrongs, I found something particularly intriguing. God seeks His children. I realized that the God I had always heard about, the One who created man, loves us so much that He would not let us wander lost in the darkness of this world. It was a joyful feeling knowing that though God is high and mighty, He was calling out to have me to Himself. Even before I could make out how much I needed Him myself, He didn't wait for me.

Before I knew He was a Father, He already walked in His capacity as a Father. That realization blew my mind. Before this time, the church was just a ritual for me, or better still a social gathering where I got to meet some of my friends. Praying and Bible reading were tasks I had no interest taking part in. But this single experience changed my life completely.

I decided that if God's love made me worth looking for, then His love was worth pursuing, worth giving myself over to. I was yet to meet love that huge, He didn't have to, yet He sought for me. Make no mistake about it, God knows exactly where you are! He wasn't looking for a missing person when He asked Adam and Eve where they were hiding. I wasn't missing either.

When we all look through our lives, we can see His love seeking us out for an amazing relationship with us. So, I became more intentional in my walk with God by putting to practice all I had learned but had never given attention. Devotions became more real. I started seeking out my bible to find out what He had for me, as an individual in a personal walk with God. Not the global church attitude I used to have. The more I did, the more the love became bigger and even more real.

I woke up one day with a verse tugging at my heart. I knew I had heard it being preached several times, but I just wasn't sure where it was. It stayed around long enough for me to know it wasn't just my thoughts. So, I went searching for it. *"...but the people that do know their God shall be strong, and do exploits..."*- Daniel 11 verse 32

Well, I found the verse but didn't know what else to do with it. Until I got to church the next Sunday. We were finishing Sunday school and there was an announcement from the Sunday school unit right after the class. "For the next one year, we will be running a series titled *Knowing God"* they said.

Instantly, the verse jumped right at me again. I was excited. There and then, I understood why my attention had been drawn to that verse. This was no longer my regular Sunday school. This was designed for me. God wanted me to know Him!

You can imagine the joy and the determination I had moving forward. God had just designed a learning year for me, and I was all set for it. I straightened up the posture of my heart, got a new journal and pen, and was set for this adventure. We moved quickly through the various attributes of God. And standing out to me much more than others was ABBA Father- God's fatherhood.

ABBA FATHER

Why would the God of the universe choose to be a Father to mortal men? To me? I didn't really understand what the role of a father was, or how a father acted. However, one thing I knew was that I had someone who I could talk to, who I could tell about all my fears, disadvantages, limitations, and insecurities.

If there was anything I couldn't share with anyone, I could share with Him. He cares that much about me. It was amazing knowing that I could do life with Him. That He is Alpha and Omega, in Him my future was secure because He does not only know the future, He is in charge of this future. Finally! Someone without limitations had my back.

While I first learned about God's reassuring love in terms of doing life and stability, over the years, I have realized that God's fatherhood meant different things to different people, especially to those who didn't have a father figure. In an interview on the King's Women Series, Sensational Nigerian Singer and photographer, TY Bello, shared her experience of encountering God as a Father in a way many kids without a father could relate to.

She lost her dad at an early age and was raised by her independent hard-working mother. Her mom covered up all the gaps; she never thought she had anything missing. Until a *Toblerone* (A Swiss chocolate bar brand) incidence caused her to have a rethink. Her friend's dad, who had recently returned from a trip, brought some Toblerone with him.

In TY Bello's words, her friend had said to her, "Toyin, you don't have a dad, who is going to buy you Toblerone?" And for the first time, she reasoned as much as her mind as a child could, "Ooh…they have something that I don't have". Today, TY Bello is glad that God was the first father-figure that was sold to her. She wanted a father, so she accepted God's invitation to be her father. She got her desires; now she had someone she could ask for Toblerone.

TY also saw girls as flowers but had gone through ugly experiences that left her feeling ugly, not the same as other girls. So, to her, that's why salvation works. She now had a daddy, and she was going to be a flower again, she was going to be a girl, she was going to be beautiful again.

One thing some people without fathers could easily find comfort in is the attribute of God as a Father. That was the case for TY Bello and I followed that same path. Unfortunately, it's not the same for everyone. Kristine Steakley in her book, *Child of Divorce, Child of God,* describes how the faithfulness of our earthly fathers influences our relationship with Abba Father.

Because we have seen our fathers leave, watch them at their worst and break their promises, we have learnt not to expect anything from them. Sometimes, we naturally extend this doubt to our relationship with God. But Abba Father reaches out to us in love over and over again. He keeps His promises and goes above and beyond.

From lover to protector, to provider, even to confidant, God's fatherhood is big enough to meet us at whatever point the void in our lives seems most pronounced. And that void is as different for each one of us just as we are. For me, it meant that irrespective of what disadvantages my upbringing may present, I was now being carried on wings bigger and stronger than my home.

And yes! I was ready for life. I gladly handed over my life as a project to God who not only created me but had my life plan in His hands. I moved away from building my life in uncertainty, fear, and limitations to building in confidence with the Father. And as I found myself in the wilderness of life, my life trailed the words of the Psalmist as he wandered all alone in the wilderness:

"When my father and my mother forsake me, then the LORD will take me up."
Psalm 27 verse 10

I had become God's own project, a life built by God.

STEPPING INTO THE FATHER'S LOVE

Take a moment to reflect on who God is to you. God is many things to us: Creator, Savior, Lord, and many others. God wants to immerse us in an experience that goes beyond what He can do to who He is. The more we open our hearts to all He is to us, the more we enjoy our relationship with Him. Every attribute of God we explore brings us into a new dimension with Him.

Imagine a child whose mother is also his class teacher. While others are limited to the teaching experience, such a child has a much richer experience. It is no mistake that God chose to be Father to the entire human race. Yes, to as many who accept Him, those who had a great upbringing, and those who didn't have the opportunity to have one.

Even though many of us go on living without Him, every day, His heart calls out to us in love. And in His reconciliation plan, He brings us not only to be at peace with Him but to know Him as our Father.

Are you ready to accept that love today? You can say this prayer:

Father, I pray in the name of Jesus, that You fill me with Your goodness and the power of your mighty love. I pray that you help me to know You as a Father. Come with Your love and heal my broken heart. Bind up my wounds and restore me in Your love.

Release a greater understanding of You in my heart as a Father who loves me and accepts me. You are a Father who wants to be close to His children? So, I pray for the opening of my heart right now to receive the Father's love. I open my heart to Your love. Thank you for Your love.

You did not send your Son to die on the cross so that I would remain in separation. I was designed to live in Your love and freely give it out. I receive it today. This is a new day with a new opportunity to love and be loved.

I thank You for it, in Jesus' name, Amen.

Get in position. Calling out for our Father is the first step in experiencing His love. We experience His love as we declare the truth that His unfailing love is here. And when we give love, we allow the Father's love to flow through us and we experience His love in a real and fulfilling way.

You are sought for, valued, and loved by your Heavenly Father.

CHAPTER EIGHT

BUILDING WITH THE FATHER

"I do not feel that I am the product of chance, a speck of dust in the universe, but someone who was expected, prepared, prefigured. In short, a being whom only a Creator could put here; and this idea of a creating hand refers to God."

~Jean-Paul Sartre

Have you ever cringed at the sight of a poorly built house, whether physically or on the screen?. Now imagine that it was a poorly built life. You are still cringing, right? As a young child, one of my outdoor activities was building sand houses with my siblings and friends. How easily my sand house crumbled! It wouldn't even allow me to fit in the stones that represented myself and my dream family.

I often watched in amazement how some of the houses built by my other playmates looked better when compared to mine. They were not the best friends because, in their bid to always have the best houses, they never showed me what to do to make my sand house better.

Many times, I would scatter everything to start all over again. I will look closely at my friends' houses and see something I didn't do or a mistake I had made. So, I will pull it all down in anger and frustration to start all over again.

It seemed I took the same approach when it came to life itself. Even as a young kid, I was dissatisfied with my life. Then, one night, I found an answer. If life made some mistakes, then maybe it was time to correct the mistake, even if I was the mistake.
I was not happy and was a little angry that evening. By bedtime I was still angry; holding onto resentments from the whooping I got from my mom for doing something wrong.

Growing up, discipline was assumed by parents to be best served by scolding, punishing, whooping or spanking. While my mom devised other ways, whooping was still a part of the mix. So, I had it all planned out in my head. It didn't take long in movies, so I figured out that should be the case here too. Mom probably wouldn't care anyway. I would slip away and by the time she finds me, I would be long gone; away from all my mom's scolding and everything I didn't want anymore.

For a while, each time my mom disciplined me, I was okay consoling myself by imagining that I had a real family that would come pick me up soon. It is funny how I never thought about my dream family when all went well except when I got into trouble with mom. I thought to myself, "If I truly belong in this family, she shouldn't make me feel this way. Why not just correct me with no discipline?" That was what I saw often on TV; parents always showed love without discipline.

There must have been a mistake somewhere. So, I spent many nights lying in bed with my eyes shut and mind far away imagining that one day my real parents would show up to pick me up. Besides, my real parents would be super-rich, prettier, live in the best houses, drive luxury cars, and have all the things I longed for.

If my mom was this tough, then there must be some mistake somewhere, there must be a nicer mom for me out there. This was my rebound strategy whenever I got disciplined or spanked by my mum in the typical African way.

However, on this particular night, it became obvious my rebound strategy wasn't working. If my magical parents were supposed to show up, why had they not shown up? Why would this linger on? If I wasn't getting my dream, I wasn't ready to continue anymore. Life was not what I wanted, there was a mistake!

So, night came and I jumped on my bed and my little self —I was about 7 years old at the time—planned to stop breathing. I had no idea what that meant or how weighty it was. However, I had learned in school and watched on the TV that breathing was the reason we stayed alive, so what a good way to put my knowledge to practice. And that I did. What I didn't know was how impossible it was to hold my breath. So, I tried once, and then the second time.

Then, my mom came into the room and did something sweet that caught my attention. She probably brought a filled kerosene lantern to our room; that was a routine every night so we wouldn't wake up in the dark all afraid. First, she prayed with us and then she turned the lantern to burn slowly, keeping it away in the corner of the room. I saw her drop the lamp and that was the last thing I knew because I slept off.

NOT A MISTAKE

"Your mom does not have a son"

I can never predict where this sentence is headed whenever someone gets to know my mom was raising only daughters.
I've had a few people ask if my father's desire for male children fueled his absence. I have always chuckled at such an African mindset. I never knew its weight until I came to meet women who struggled with their father's rejection, just for one reason. They were girls; their fathers wanted boys.

Recently, I saw a home birth video. Although it wasn't my first time seeing a birth clip, this was a little different and it stirred some deep thoughts. A mother had just given birth in a tub in her own home, supported by her midwife, doula, and partner.

Both mom and baby were spending a few moments resting and bonding. The child, who I imagined could not understand all the changes he was experiencing, curled up closely in his mother's bosom for some comfort. The baby's dad came on the scene, cut the baby's cord, and lifted the baby from the tub.

The cries returned once again, and I looked closely at the child. I thought to myself, this boy never chose any of his present circumstances. He didn't choose his family, gender, skin color, nails, or shape. Not only his present circumstances, but some of his experiences in life are also events he would have no absolute power over. The height he grows to, the love or hurt he receives from his family, all are outside his control. I guess if he had the power to choose, he would select for himself pleasant experiences and avoid a bunch of experiences he would rather not face.

Just like the little boy, we are all born dependent, clueless, without an understanding of life and its purpose. We do not choose the circumstances of our birth, the homes we are born into, our gender, race, and so many other things.

Beyond what happens at birth, we also run through various experiences we would rather not be a part of like disabilities, death or separation of our parents, instability in our countries, amongst other things. Today, the uncertainties, ills, and pain in this world have made many believe they are mere products of chance in a disoriented world. Ask the boy moving from one foster home to the other, the girl who just lost her amazing father, the young woman who has been sexually abused, or the young man in a war-torn country: nothing makes sense. They feel like a number in a world they know nothing about.

Like the sands on the seashore, it seems we are very insignificant in this grand scheme called life. Even the best of men have moments where they have questioned their essence in this world. Daily, many battle suicidal tendencies because of this confusion, feeling of worthlessness, and a lack of understanding of our essence.

We have all been there, whether in big ways or small moments of life. Those seasons when we ask ourselves, *what is life all about? Why am I even here? What does my life amount to?* When we look at some people, it is easy to conclude that there is an essence to their existence on earth. They seem to have beautiful and meaningful lives. Then, we look at our lives and we just can't say the same thing about ourselves.

As I watched this new baby, I understood he will go through times where he needs answers to the purpose of his existence; a rescue from confusion and worthlessness life throws at him; times when life becomes a puzzle and the missing parts do not fit the pieces at hand.

My thoughts were interrupted as something important happened next. His father lifted him from the tub right into the air and began to pray. At that moment, I felt the boy being returned into the hands of the One who created him; the One who knows all the details of his life and the purpose behind each of those details. A place where all the missing pieces can be found. The only place where it all makes sense, where we get an understanding of the purpose of our lives and the strength we need throughout all our years in life.

IS THERE A RIGHT WAY TO BUILD?

Dubbed the worst building in the world or hotel of doom, the Ryugyong Hotel is famous for the wrong reasons. When construction began on the building in 1987, the Ryugyong Hotel, the world's 22nd largest skyscraper, was designed to become an impressive masterpiece.

North Korea poured heavily into Ryugyong to achieve this masterpiece, costing more than two percent of its gross domestic product. Decades later, this hotel was yet to open its doors to guests and is likely to remain this way for a long time or forever.

Construction on the Hotel of Doom stopped a few years after it started, picked up a little much later but over the last few years, things have remained quiet on this site. It is rumored that North Korea ran out of money, or that the building was engineered improperly and could never be occupied. Whatever the case may be with Ryugyong Hotel, this project tells that building requires a lot of work!

Those years when I sat in my mom's small space for her produce, I would sometimes see people who seemed to be doing fine driving past or stopping by to get something. Once they were gone, I would get back into my zone of imagination. Imagining how all of life's pieces will fit together; imagining how I could pull together all the resources I had to magically build a beautiful life.

Back then, if I was ever asked what was needed to build a beautiful life, I guess it would easily come down to one major thing - money. I watched wealthy people drive around in their expensive cars, good clothes and believed they had the best lives. It was therefore logical to assume all I needed to have a beautiful life was money.

I also thought I had figured out society's blueprint for a good life: going to school, getting a good job, and getting married—especially to a wealthy person. Those were keys sold to us as the required ingredients for building a great life. From home it was about going to school; at church, more about prayers; and in movies, it was more about getting married to someone on the upper rung of the social ladder.

So, I appreciated my friends with wealthy parents. They were all set, it looked like they had it all. Rich parents meant good schools, even private universities, and other resources that seem to put them at an advantage. But since I already had God in my corner, I was content with my journey, but I wasn't expecting much from life. My life's lens remained blinded by my limitations.

As I grew older, I started to realize many things weren't adding up. Wealthy people, career executives, married people, those who attended the best schools or had the best opportunities in life still didn't seem out rightly happy. Many who ticked these boxes were still at a loss of what made life beautiful. Then I read about suicidal stories of celebrities and I was dazed, *"what else do they want?"*

Around this period, I continued to invest in my relationship with God and to grow in my knowledge of God's attributes. I got to know one truth that put me at ease about building a beautiful life for myself. *For every house is built by someone, but He who builds all things is God (*Hebrews 3:4 KJV*)*

A little confusing at first, but then I came to understand it better through the light from another verse of the bible; *Except the Lord build the house, they labor in vain that build it (*Psalm 127:3 KJV*).* Then I thought, maybe that was the answer to all that wasn't adding up in the lives of the celebrities around me. The difference really was about who was in charge of building their lives.

"For we are God's masterpiece. He has created us anew in Christ Jesus, so we can do the good things he planned for us long ago" – Ephesians 2:10 NLT

The tents of every successful life are held together by the right cords in the right places. If we are to live the life God has designed for us, then we have the responsibility of building that life on His terms. Living out God's plan for our lives hinges on our ability to pull together different resources that build us into the person that God desires us to be.

If we are His masterpiece, then He has the blueprint, not the society. And just as our life's purposes and callings differ from one another, so also does our blueprint differ. What we need to build our lives are unique to us as we are unique to the world.

Without the right structures, we will only go on to live underdeveloped lives and never reach the full potential God has designed us for. Potential continues to remain what it is—untapped and unacknowledged—because the structures needed to harness that potential are not available.
And like my sand house couldn't hold my dreams, many people remain unable to accomplish the dream they have in them in their lifetime.

There were other resources needed for my sand house apart from the sand. I also needed water and stones. And while I lacked the knowledge needed to put my resources together to build, my playmates did. This lack put me at a disadvantage, no matter how hard I tried, I could not build a great sand house.

This is what disadvantages do to us; they rob us of the essentials we need in building and make it difficult for us to incorporate the right structures into our lives. It is not always a lack. Sometimes, disadvantages mess up with our structures by putting in the wrong things we do not need which are deleterious to us.

CHAPTER NINE

HOMEMADE

Love is said to be homemade, happiness too. But it's not just those two. A lot more than we acknowledge about our lives are homemade. I'm a homemade girl; seasoned in my mom's pot of love. Starting from my looks down to many other things. If you know, you know. If you don't, I'll tell you a quick story. A few years back, it was a tense morning at work and the pressure was at its peak. It was yet another visit by government officials, the second in two years.

The last time, we barely pulled through, so this was of utmost importance to us. Being pulled aside by a member of the panel was the last thing I wanted after the hectic preparation. So, I was agitated when a woman on the panel pulled me aside for some questioning. My mind raced about the possible questions she may ask me. So, when she asked, "How is your mom?" I had to give her a second glance.

"Like seriously? What has my mom got to do with you or what we had going on?" I thought to myself. "She is fine", I managed to mutter. My brain was fired up wondering what the connection between this strange lady and my mom was. "Please give me her number", she added. "My mom's number"? I repeated. Her response was yes. I still couldn't find a justifiable reason to give out my mom's number, but this woman had my adult self lost for a while.

"Okay", I said after thinking it through for a moment. I gave her the number, she saved the number on her phone and walked away. Why on earth would a stranger ask for my mom's number? Well, she seemed harmless. Maybe she had met my mom on the other side of the campus. My mom worked at the same campus that I worked in, and she sometimes had to deal with academic guests. There could be no other connection. "I'll give my mom a heads-up anyway," I concluded as I walked away.

I completely forgot to give my mom an update all through the rest of the hectic day. When I caught up with her later that evening, I told her about the strange woman who had asked for her number. "Oh, Ayo", she said. No, I am not talking about any Ayo. I repeated what I had said. "Yes, it is Ayo," mom insisted. When she saw the confusion in my face, she quickly added more information about Ayo. "She's the daughter of Professor A in Ibadan."

Oh! It all made sense now. "What? How come she knew I was your daughter? She had never met me before now." I retorted "Well, she said she knew who you were my daughter the moment she laid her eyes on you" mom replied. I shook my head in disbelief. "Is it that deep?" I joked with my mom.

Professor A had been my mom's boss more than 2 decades before that year. Ayo was only a young girl back then. Ayo and her other siblings would usually spend their after-school hours in their dad's office. My mom gladly took up the task of caring for them during these long hours, ensuring they were fed and that they settled in properly.

When it was time to get married, my mom got a transfer from her university to another state to join my dad. She moved an hour away, but with the demands of her new family and dad's subsequent transfer to other states, she saw less of Ayo and her family. Communication was also not as easy as it is now.

Mom, of course, told us about this wonderful family. They asked about us too and she always relayed their messages. A few times, she had also traveled on a few occasions to celebrate with them, especially as the kids got married. I was accustomed to people asking if she was my mom. This one was on another level.

Even more interesting are those who mention how much I did not just look like my mom, but I also act like her. It is often said that children are mirrors of their homes, but beyond the physical features, how much do we reflect?

THE HOME IS PRIMARY; GOD MADE IT SO

"Home is where the heart is." – Pliny the Elder

In 2018, an American poker player, Rich Alati, stretched the human mind to unusual territories. He decided to spend 30 days alone and in total darkness for a bet of US$100,000. Since it sounded like cool money to make for just chilling out alone for 30 days, Rich decided it was worth a try. He was kept in a small, completely dark room with access to a bed, fridge, and bathroom.

However, even with all the resources he needed to survive, Alati couldn't last the month. After 20 days, he negotiated his release accepting a payout of US$62,400. Humans are social beings. God did not design man to live solitary lives, rather, He designed us for fellowship with each other and our Creator.

People who have satisfying relationships with family, friends, and their community are happier, have fewer health problems, and live longer. From interactions with strangers at the mall to colleagues, friends, family, our lives are built around the people we live with.

Our first social relationships are found in the home. Many of us are so in love with our homes! What feelings does the word home evoke within us? For many, and that includes me, home means not one, but many things. More than a building, yard, wood, or bricks, the home is a haven and a comfort zone. A place to live with our families, enjoy with friends, build memories, and ultimately our future.

The home is not just a product of chance and unlike some other social institutions formed by man, the original idea of the home can be traced to God. After God placed man in the garden, God showed us a pattern of social interaction: first is marriage, the family, and finally society.

Every other institution comes after the home. God ordained that for every new individual born to the world, the home is the first place of contact, providing nurture and care that the young life needs. God made the home a primary contact for every individual, placing solitary individuals in families, not in schools or churches.

I spent 4 years in an agro-based institution and saw first-hand how greenhouses operated. The home, in many ways, is similar to a greenhouse. A greenhouse allows for greater control over the growing environment of young plants; from regulating warmth and humidity to providing the right nutrients that the plants need to grow. And that's what a home does; creating a safe environment for a child while nurturing the child to grow and be prepared for the world.

THE HOME, GOD'S FIRST WORKMAN

I grew up with 3 amazing ladies, they were all my sisters. We shared all of our childhood. Growing up, we were often told how much we looked like each other. Though the degree of resemblance was not the same. But really, we were alike in many ways. We were of similar heights, complexions, and sizes, spoke the same language, ate similar food, watched the same TV shows, and many more things.

As we grew older, attended different schools, got on different career paths, changed environments, and lifestyles, I have come to realize how much the similarities have started to dissolve. Our preferences on so many things have become as varied as our experiences as we journeyed through life.

Despite this, some of the things that are deep-rooted in our identities remain the same. Our preference for food, fashion, among other things may change; but our faith, respectful demeanour, and other core values all stand the same. It reflects one thing; the experiences we had growing in our home.

Although we are reflections of our experiences and relationships all through our lives, the home is the starting point. Indeed, it takes many workmen to build us into God's plans and agenda, but the home occupies a special place.

God appointed the home to be the very first workman. From God's dealing with His people, we see that beyond primary care, God has an agenda for making the home the first of His workmen. Our homes represent the very first influence over our lives, and parents as the single greatest influence on us.

Home and family are the most important and influential institutions of society—educational as well as religious. Teachers, universities, and schools are important, but more important are the homes from which teachers come. Classmates are influential, but more influential are the homes from which the classmates come. The restored church proclaims that the family may be eternal. It is only God-centered family living that helps us to reach these goals.

Interestingly, to allow the home to exert its greatest influence, we arrive in our homes at a time when we are most impressionable. By the time we were born, some influences were already established. Studies have shown that development starts from the womb and the home's influence starts as early as this stage. Beyond birth and early life, the child-parent relationship continues to be a major influence on most aspects of a child's life even unto adulthood.

I love to say that as God steers the ship of humanity, the home is the wheel. Our societies are a product of what transpires in a home. What God desires to see in project humanity reflects first from the home into the society. Biblical genealogy provides a weighty revelation on the importance of the home to God. We see that God runs the affairs of a man's life not only by today's circumstances but by His eternal plans. And that eternal plan involves an entire family or lineage running far beyond the number of years a man can spend on earth. Each man carries in him the plan of God for his generation.

For example, the eternal redemption plan rested on the lineage of David years before Christ was born. God's agenda for our generation has our parts in it established in our homes.

THE ASSIGNMENT AND OPPOSITION

In building, every workman is tasked with a particular assignment that contributes to the overall big picture desired by the master builder. The task God has for the home is exemplified in the life of Abraham and his household. In Genesis 18:19, God explicitly found in Abraham a workman needed to fulfill His plans:

"For I have chosen him, that he may command his children and his household after him to keep the way of the Lord by doing righteousness and justice, so that the Lord may bring to Abraham what he has promised him."

As God led the Israelites out of bondage, He commanded them to teach their children about Him and all He had done for them. God's plan didn't end with the current generation, he desired that the generations to come would continue to uphold all His commandments and align with His agenda over the nation. There was only one way that this could happen. They needed to be taught about God and His special dealings with the people of Israel.

We are God's heritage. God designed the home as His primary tool for executing His influence on earth through man, just as God desired when He made man. He places children in families and provides parents with the guidance needed on how they are to be raised and prepared for His purpose and glory. The goal of godly parenting is to raise children who know and honor God with their lives.

Truly, parents do not entirely determine how we will turn out. Many factors external to both the child and family can influence the way they develop. However, while external factors also play their roles, the home remains the first influence we are exposed to and becomes the very core and foundation of our personalities. A tree determines to a large extent what its fruits look like. It is very easy to trace the outcomes of our lives, bitter or sweet, to the trees we come from.

Building in God's kingdom is not without an opposing plan. Because the home is the main vehicle for the propagation of the commandment of God and Christ's testimony, we can imagine that the home is also a prime target for the enemy.

After all, we know that if one generation can fail in their responsibility of propagating God's agenda to the next, then the enemy has succeeded in this battle. This attack on the home takes different forms from one generation to the other. In past generations, marriages and homes were plagued by child marriages, cousin marriages, and ill-treatment of women and children.

However, in these modern times, the home continues to be weakened by newer perspectives and definitions of what the home should look like. It is no surprise that of all the social institutions, the home is the most threatened institution.

There has been a lot of public mockery on the institution of marriage, the bedrock of a home. Can the home still fulfill its assignment of building the next generation for God? We know that because the home is dear to God's heart and His purpose, it is a prime target for the devil. However, it is also God's prime target for protection.

Many of the ills that befall the home directly or indirectly seek to incapacitate the home from fulfilling its God-given agenda of raising the next generation to know God. The death of parents, separation, divorce, the rise in parenting without marriage, among others are some of the tools that the enemy uses to engage the home in warfare.

All these negative events seek to reduce the workmen building a life at a critical moment, limiting the impact that two people can have to one person's impact in as many homes as possible. When the enemy succeeds in distracting the home from this noble assignment of building lives, the result is what we see in the society; broken and hurting individuals that cannot contribute positively to the society, but only give the brokenness and pain they carry.

CHAPTER TEN

BETTER THAN HOMEMADE

Is anything better than homemade? It is almost a unanimous agreement that everything is better when homemade. Maybe like me, you've always dreamt of making your homemade meal from scratch to finish, but that is still a dream that is yet to come through. Because sometimes, try hard as you might want to, your perfect meal is just never complete without that special treat from the store.

Many times, with a full home-made meal, I still buy that perfect side dish not only because it's not possible to make it at home, but just because I still can't beat the taste they have to offer. Do you sometimes make the excuse of having a balanced diet the reason to get that extra side dish? I do that all the time, betraying my home-made goals and I know I'm not alone.

Moving away from food to a building, even in this age where everyone has become a DIY (Do It Yourself) expert, it is almost an absolute impossibility to build a house without any help. Deciding to DIY can sometimes create an absolute mess, a disaster, and a waste of time and money. We all learn when to put down the tools and call in a professional.

Simply put, the act of building is a collective effort. I sometimes think of our lives in the light of a building project. The best building projects may be conceived in the heart of one person, but it usually takes the efforts of many experts to finish the work. The same thing goes for us, we are a product of the efforts of so many people: parents, relatives, teachers, mentors, and many more.

Our homes as the first workman lay the foundation, but other workmen contribute to erecting other structures. What world would we have today, if all we had to instruct, teach, guide, and mentor us are our parents only? My mother had a great influence on my life, but I wouldn't be where I am today or hope for a greater future if all I had was her.

Growing up, I had Uncle S. At a younger age, I didn't even know he wasn't my mom's biological brother. He was that engaged with us. My mom shared much later that she got to know him when he was an undergraduate in the campus where my mom worked. I learned a whole lot from him.

The first of such lessons that I remember was unforgettable teaching on how to read the clock and interpret the time accurately. I had been battling with my homework from school on how to tell the time. I barely understood the process but got the homework done anyway.

The next day, he came to the house with a clock he made himself. He had made this clock with some colorful cardboard and called me as soon as he got into the house to start his teaching. The clock was so beautiful, and I was super excited and fascinated. By the end of that lesson, I could look away from the beautiful cardboard clock to the giant wall clock in our living room and say the time with super confidence.

In addition to helping me navigate through tough school tasks, he was also my cheerleader when I brought home my school report cards. I was always so excited to show him how well I had done in school and he seemed to believe in me too.

Beyond helping with school tasks, I also learned very basic life lessons from him. My mom once informed him I stole her money. He made me understand why that was so bad. My mom had repeated loudly what the church had always said about stealing, but I couldn't see it. Uncle S. had a conversation about it instead and immediately, I could see what I wasn't able to see previously.

I also fondly remember two of my tutors. We call them lesson teachers; they were both young men with so much desire to have their students transformed. They would come to our house and would teach with all their hearts. We had a bunch of them, but these two had so much passion that was enough to set my little heart on fire. I still see one of them regularly. He hasn't changed, still very passionate and proud of us all.

One of God's biggest investments in my teen and young adult years was my Pastor and spiritual father who sacrificed day and night so I could know God for myself and have a personal relationship with God.

As I moved away from home to the university and unto other things, I have always been blessed with people who genuinely desire and invest in my becoming a better person. Like the biblical reference of a hidden treasure that even I am unable to see, these people help uncover the gold in me.

THE HIDDEN WINDOW

I first heard about the concept of the hidden window from my amazing mentor. The hidden window is one of the four quadrants of the Johari window—a practical tool to illustrate and improve self-awareness. The hidden window represents that part of us that remain invisible to us but is often visible to the people around us. While that may mean our character or personality, good or bad, sometimes, it may mean the potentials that are hidden within layers of our disadvantages, limitations, insecurities and all the negative or wrong energy that we carry.

Blessed are some eyes because they see! Sometimes, these eyes see potentials that are hidden from us, from our parents and family, from all the people that have known us all our lives. They are not only able to see it, many times, it means they are also willing to invest in us to manifest that potential that they have seen.

I will use the story of Deshauna Barber, an ex beauty queen, motivational speaker, and captain as an example. In a Goalcast interview, Deshauna Barber recounts her life-changing encounter with a total stranger In Target. Before this meeting, Deshauna had worked as a salesgirl in Target, living the only life she believed she could have. The best of plans she had for herself was to go into her sophomore year and become a military officer until she met someone who saw not just a salesgirl but a beauty queen.

This stranger provided Deshauna with all the resources and encouragement she needed to go on to her very first pageant. And she stood by Deshauna all through her years of trials and failure, all because she believed in Deshauna. She saw the potential no single person around her could see and was ready to give it all it needed to let that potential find full expression.

Like Deshauna, a few years ago, I was working on my Ph.D. research in Nigeria. I struggled so much with funding and I tried very hard to secure one. One day, someone told me straight away, "You could get a fully-funded international Ph.D. scolarship. It's a competitive process, but you have what it takes to get it." It was a long journey, but I tried and got it.

Not all treasures are silver and gold. *We have this treasure in earthen vessels, that the excellency of the power may be of God, and not of us* (2 Corinthians 4:7, KJV).

Treasures put in there by our maker Himself. Blessed are those whose parents start-up this discovery early on. But what of those with missing parents?

With all these treasures hidden underneath the rubbles of our personality and struggles, God blesses us with people who are not blinded by our weaknesses and limitations. They are still able to look beyond the pile of rubble around us to help us discover and unleash our best selves. And sometimes, those people can be total strangers, like it was in Deshauna's case.

God shows His faithfulness to us and His plans for our lives by providing people who can see the potential in our lives. Not only are they able to see the treasures God has placed in our lives, but they are also willing to work with us to transform the very unrefined us into beautiful, magnificent edifices. Some model the right way of life in different contexts e.g. marriage, finance, career, etc.

The Scripture is filled with many examples of people who contributed to the lives of others one way or the other. In the words of renowned preacher Joel Osteen, *"God puts people in our lives on purpose so we can help them succeed and help them become all He created them to be.*

Most people will not reach their full potential without somebody else believing in them."

There is a reason why God moves your heart toward a specific person and a reason why you get attached to certain people more than others. When I look back, there's not one person I got attached to who didn't have something valuable to teach me or who didn't play a major role in my life.

They come into our lives as mentors, coaches, and friends; in different shades but serving one purpose—to help uncover the greatness in our lives. Sometimes, we seek them out, other times they find us out. Either way, God can bring us into connections with such people, help us identify them, and work with them as we rely on His grace in our journey through life.

NEW BIRTH, NEW FAMILY

My love for babies goes beyond the average and I think I should be on record as a lover of babies. So, you can imagine how fulfilling it was for me to do some neonatal care related research for my graduate degree. On one of those days when I was carrying out my research, I walked through the neonatal unit to complete my task for the day.

I noticed a room with nothing, but one cot and basic supplies such as food. The room didn't have any of the features that other rooms in the ward had. On subsequent days, I noticed there was a baby there who was quite big. She could sit, so she was not a neonate and was older than the unit. Out of curiosity, I asked my clinical advisor about the big baby in the neonatal unit.

She simply mentioned a typical medical language that took me some seconds to understand. She then informed me the baby was healthy and was not supposed to be in the ward. However, the baby also had no home to stay. Why would a baby not have a home?

Apparently, the baby's mother had slipped out of the hospital after delivery leaving the baby all by herself. The baby was then transferred to the neonatal unit so she could at least get some care. And that was not all, the baby was super lucky. An eminent personality in the community had decided to adopt her. So, they were waiting for the legal process to be completed, and then they would be able to welcome her to the family.

As I left my advisor's office, it all began to make some sense. A few days before then, some nurses in the ward were feeding and taking care of the baby girl and telling her how lucky she was. They were telling her how beautiful the rest of her life would be and how she would not come into a place of lack.

A fed baby is a happy baby, so the little girl was full of giggles and coos even though she didn't understand what they said. I remember telling myself, maybe she intuitively felt she was in a better place!

Every child of God is supposed to be excited at the very thought of being adopted by our heavenly Father. So, while we have an earthly family here on earth, we are also part of God's heavenly family; a bona fide member. Our salvation is complete, every legal process for our adoption has been finalized. Glory to God! We don't have to be in a waiting room. The moment we choose to give our lives to Christ, we are immediately brought into His big family.

The church shows us that the Christian faith is a 'together' faith. And of course, we are in a better place. While God takes care of each of His creatures including man, His own family has a special place in His heart.

All of us, regardless of our circumstances in life, are "fellow citizens with God's people and members of

God's household" as Paul says in Ephesians 2:19. You and I have been adopted into God's family and have become God's children (Romans 8:16).

In his book, *Now That You Are Saved,* Reinhard Bonnke, a world-leading evangelist, describes the life of any man who receives God's gift of salvation.
He describes it as the actual moment when someone is told that they have won a large cash prize in a competition. Sometimes, we do not fully understand what has happened to us. But one thing stands true, we won a great deal.

As we begin to understand and acknowledge what has happened to us, we begin to see the limitless and inexhaustible gifts that we have received; and that includes the gift of a family. No matter what our backgrounds are; the deep rot in our homes, or if we didn't have one at all, salvation brings us into a brand-new family with people who love us with Abba's kind of love.

HE'S GOT THE WHOLE WORLD

I'm taken down memory lane to those moments when we sang heartily "He's got the whole world in His hands…" I would usually imagine how big that hand must be. I never imagined in my tiny heart that it meant more than the blue globe that I could see on the wall. He has the whole world, so how does that count now?

The song is a reminder that God is in control of all aspects of His creation and we should take comfort in His presence.
From the birds in the air to tiny babies and grown-up men, presidents, and world leaders, everything has been, remains, and will always lie in His hands.

So, we know that God has adopted us into His own big family. We are recipients of His many wonderful plans for His family. We can conveniently list out the benefits we are receiving from this big family. It is easier to relate to people of faith. We have found a comfort zone.

However, our world is much bigger than our close-knit Christian comfort zone. Even when we step out of all we have known, when we chart new territories, move on to new locations, meet people we have never known; one thing stands true - God reigns and rules sovereign over every niche in this world. Even outside the Christian family.

No event, no persons, systems, or location is outside the sphere of His influence. Nothing is too big to confuse God or cause a disruption in heaven.
God knows perfectly well I wasn't going to have my dad around for that. He catered and is catering for that in all ways known and unknown to me. The same thing for everyone else, God was aware of the ride across the ocean of life and has catered adequately for that even before the storms arose.

MORE THAN OUR HOMES

Barack Obama, Dr. Ben Carson, Olympic swimmer Michael Phelps; these names have one thing in common. They were raised by single parents. These are a few among very famous examples. There are many individuals out there that have a reality that looks nothing like the challenging upbringing they had.

While the stats do show that being raised in a difficult or non-traditional family increases the likelihood of poorer life outcomes in young people, there are examples around us of people who rose above the odds. Some have experienced extreme poverty, war, abuse, trafficking, and all sorts of unimaginable vices, yet they evolved beautifully from the same circumstances that denied others their dreams.

We may see the deficits in our foundations that robbed us of the opportunity to build our lives right. We can also see how faulty foundations in our lives have put us on the wrong path. However, these examples remind us that we can rise above our backgrounds, refusing to let them dictate the rest of our lives.

The term *broken home* is limited to the circumstance of our upbringing, not our identities. The choices our parents made may have caused us to grow in a broken home or no home at all, however, it shouldn't leave us broken. Holding on to being born out of wedlock, being raised by a single parent or an orphan as an excuse or an explanation to our limitations and failures is simply denying God's providence and sovereignty; and that's not a good place to be.

CHAPTER ELEVEN

MEN ARE SCUM: THE STRONG WOMEN TRIBE

Three words that leave trails of reactions right after them: *Men are scum*! Not many know the history connected with these words, but I am happy to share some part of it that I stumbled on. The word scum refers to dirt or grime and I thought that was all there was to it. Much speculation has surrounded the 'radical feminist' meaning or origin of the word SCUM. I was surprised when I got to know that not only was SCUM an acronym, there was a SCUM manifesto. Yes, you read that right, a manifesto.

Some decades back, in the sixties precisely, a famous radical feminist, Valerie Solana, founded an organization called the Society for Cutting Up Men (SCUM). Around the same time, Solana self-published her best-known work, the SCUM Manifesto.

In this manifesto, Solana addressed a certain group of women who were the so-called "scum" of society. She encouraged that they act like "dominant, secure, self-confident, nasty, violent, selfish, independent, proud, thrill-seeking, free-wheeling, arrogant females". They envisioned a world without men, calling on "civic-minded, responsible, thrill-seeking females" to "overthrow the government, eliminate the money system, institute complete automation and eliminate the male sex."[7]

SCUM Manifesto – which predicted ATMs, test-tube babies, the Internet, and artificial insemination long before they existed – has sold more copies, and has been translated into more languages, than nearly all other feminist texts of it's time. Up until her death, Solana continued to believe she could change the world with her SCUM Manifesto.

Weird extremist, you may say, right? If it helps to give a better perspective on how Solana's mind was wired, Solana had a turbulent childhood. She was said to have been regularly sexually abused by her father and later on by her alcoholic grandfather. At 15, she was already homeless, had a child she had to give up for adoption, and later had to support herself through begging and prostitution.

If I had read the SCUM manifestation or met Solana in the few teen years I had the mind of a SCUM member, I would have had a good reason to explain why I started to drift along that way. But no, no one enrolled me in that school of thought, it was just a natural response to the events going on around me. When I was done with high school, I spent one year waiting to get through with my admission into the university.

That meant that I had more time to spend at home, more time with my mom and other women. In that season, it seemed most women in my immediate sphere had the same story to tell. Tales of abandonment and negligence were a common story I heard over and over in that season.
Thinking about it now, I doubt if that was an absolute reflection of what was going on in society. It was probably a consequence of being around women brought together because of the similarity of their stories and experiences.

After brooding over these women's cases, I decided without consulting or sharing with anyone that I wasn't going to be a victim like they were. By the way, one or two of them stood out to me as warriors. They were typical examples of the stereotypical strong black women - women who are never broken or affected by the storms of life; standing strong come rain or sunshine.

One was a director; soon she fit perfectly into the definition of a 'role model' we were always taught to have. I loved her carriage, ambiance, beauty, style, and how she forged ahead despite her 'not so great' home situation.

So, I conjured in my head a plan to be the strong black woman, not the victimized silenced one. I identified quickly the tools that would feed my aspirations: a good degree, a great career, an influential position, and of course, lots of money.

Marriage was on the list, but not to be taken seriously. It was just for the reasons these women endured; to have kids.

A woman's first idea of a man is in her father. His influence in his daughter's life shapes her, not only her self-esteem, self-image, and confidence, it also influences her opinions of men. A man serves as "a template for all male figures – teachers, boyfriends, her husband, uncles, and even God himself – in a daughter's life. Research bears this out, revealing that early sexual activity and teenage pregnancy are more common in girls who grow up with absent fathers.

Poor father-daughter relationships result in difficulty in trusting and communicating with men and with forming lasting relationships. Many hold on to the scum agenda that it becomes their core. Thankfully, God interrupted my journey by blessing me with couples who modeled the right home to me. Today, I am off the scum path to helping young women understand God's truth about the home. Otherwise, without knowing why, my scum agenda was setting me up at a disadvantage even in my journey.

The disadvantaged mind is just one out of the many conditions we get exposed to when we don't have the experience of two healthy and loving parents. Our experiences make our minds a fertile ground for all sorts of wrong mindsets on relationships, finances, spirituality among others.

MINDSET MAKEOVER

Makeovers! One big word in our age. My first experience with makeovers was unforgettable. "Is this you?" Everyone knew what I looked like, so it was hard to convince them I was the same person in the picture. I was just a regular powder and lip gloss girl, until my first makeover. That year, I volunteered to be a model for a friend advertising her makeup skills.

After an hour of face beating, nice jewelry, and a headgear, I couldn't even recognize the person in the mirror anymore. The pictures captured the look perfectly as the few people who saw them much later on my phone couldn't believe I was the same person in the photograph. It turned out gorgeous. I looked just like the brides I had seen in beautiful magazines.

As beautiful as it was, that was where it all ended. Immediately after the pictures were taken, I walked straight to the bathroom to wash my face. That event sapped out all the little energy reserve I had left from my busy lab day. I needed to sleep and there was no way that makeover could remain a part of my day.

Have you ever seen people before and after makeovers? Makeovers are great; their transforming power is huge. But, makeovers don't last forever, I really wish they did. We pay more for any product that promises a long-lasting effect. By the way, don't we all agree that in today's world, nothing lasts forever?

That is what society says. However, the Bible's standpoint is that only three things last forever: faith, hope, and love. *"Three things will last forever--faith, hope, and love"* I Corinthians 13:13. These three things have one thing in common; they are matters of the heart. Unseen, yet they remain powerful forces that beat in our hearts and hold our lives together.

This trio in the life of anyone produces more transformation than any makeover can.
Faith taught my heart the truth about God and the essence of life. I believed in God for who He is and what He means to me in every single way. It healed my heart from its sense of worthlessness, confusion, and weariness.

Hope taught me to hold on to God's grand plans for my life. I learned to ditch limitations and barriers because my heavenly Father runs the show. Love taught me that no one man or woman is scum. It healed my heart of its selfish tendencies. I realized I was on the same path that I had judged: a selfish life led far away from God's love.

Did it happen instantly? No, it didn't. But day in and day out, as I open my heart to God, His words, His people, these ever-lasting trio continue to work within me to birth a new me, that is a long-lasting makeover. No limitations, no resentments, no baggage!

Do you need a makeover that is enough to last your lifetime? Make these ever-lasting trio the foundation of your makeover kit. *Faith, hope, and love* are delivered to our heart through various means, but they are sourced from only one person - God.

THE SWEET BITTER PILL

If there's anyone who portrayed the best way of relating with family after hurtful events, then the first person I will put on that list is Joseph. He was born into a great family, but Joseph didn't experience a pleasant life even in his home. His father's love for him, as well as his dream of ruling over his brothers, stirred his brothers into bitterness and selling him off to slavery.

Although he was hated and treated unfairly by his brothers, Joseph continued to align himself with God and God's purposes for his life. Gradually, Joseph came into God's plan for his life and nation. He was at a good place to get revenge when his brothers needed help. However, Joseph's understanding fueled his forgiving attitude towards his brothers.

It is very easy to become resentful amid our pains and trials. Yes, our present unpleasant circumstances now may have been caused by the poor choices of our parents and family, but none of it is outside the knowledge of God.
We understand that the challenges in our home are part of the ploys of the enemy to destroy and ruin the awesome plans God has in store for us. And we do know that God is in our pains and trials, doing great work in us. He can provide us with love, care, help, and support in areas and times when we need them.

Our fixation on the faults of our parents and families says that we are yet to understand the plan against God's very first workmen, the home. It shows we are yet to hand our lives over to God and that we still see our lives as dependent on our home. When we begin to see things in the right perspective, every form of bitterness and hatred begins to melt away.

These days, I wish my dad knew better than to make the poor decisions he made years ago. He missed out on all the wonderful growing moments of his four beautiful daughters. While everyone has chosen to forget the past and move on, those years of absence cannot be recovered, we can only attempt to make up for them.

I am confronted with these questions a lot: *where's your dad now? Did you ever get to see him again? Do you have any relationship with him?* After the glimpse I had in his office, I never laid my eyes on him till I was out of college. We lived apart while my mom raised me. Today, I have a working relationship with my dad and I keep working on it to make it better.

With the lens of love, I can see past his actions to the goal of the enemy in destroying his home and children. And of course, the enemy failed woefully! God was there for us all through! Why then would I ever stick to resentment? God covered all the gaps. Yes, I wish I had my dad's love, care, and attention during my growing years, but I didn't. I'm glad that God did take care of me as He promised in Psalm 27:10.

Sometimes, the enemy flashes the memory of the pains from the past, stirring up bitterness, anger, and fault finding, but God's love wipes the slate clean each time. Over and over, I have refused to trade the consciousness of God's grace and love for any form of resentment.

Forgiveness is one struggle a lot of people still deal with today. For many, the pains of their parents' mess still live with them. Forgiveness is, however, not an option, but rather a command requiring obedience. God has called us to forgive those who hurt us, just as He has forgiven us.

Forgiveness may not come naturally to us, but as we accept God's love for our lives, we begin to reckon with His graciousness more than the recklessness of our parents. When unforgiveness persists, we can always pray and ask God for the grace to forgive. And instead of bitterness or resentment, His love and peace can begin to flood our hearts.

CHAPTER TWELVE

BUILT FOR GLORY

The human mind has no limits! It is amazing how people wake up with lofty ideas and dreams. I guess one very good day, the ruler of Dubai was hit by an idea that had dropped in his mind several decades ago. Just that this time around, he meant it and was sure to follow up with the idea to completion; that was how the tallest building in the world came to be.

Burj Khalifa – Does this word ring a bell? Or are you a witness of the wonder the word holds?
The Burj Khalifa is currently the tallest building in the world. The idea of building Burj Khalifa was inspired by the visit of Dubai's ruler to the Empire State Building, the tallest building at that time in the 1960s.

Dubai is crowned as the "City of Gold". The idea for the building came at a time when an oil boom in the United Arab Emirates produced unprecedented wealth for the small Gulf nation. The country wanted to lighten its reliance on oil and make tourism one of the key industries.

Dubai also wanted to improve its reputation in the world, and to capture the attention of the world. And so, they put into effect a plan to turn the city into the world's top tourist destination. That plan included the building of outlandish landmarks like the Burj Khalifa.

Today, Burj Khalifa, the tallest manmade structure in the world, is the ultimate symbol of glitz and glamor. Towering over the city, at 2,717 feet tall with 160 floors, the Burj Khalifa attracts almost 2 million tourists each year.
Burj Khalifa typifies what it means for a building to reflect the glory and glamor of a country. The building was built for that reason, to fulfill Dubai's desire to tell the world about itself. Years after Burj Khalifa, another mega building, much taller than Burj Khalifa is under construction and the world awaits the unveiling of yet another glory from Dubai.

I have always imagined that on the sixth day of creation, the entire heavens awaited the unveiling of this masterpiece that God had spent the day working on. He created this masterpiece in a very special way, in His image and likeness. He created us for His glory.

"Thus says the Lord, "Bring my sons from afar and my daughters from the end of the earth, everyone who is called by my name, whom I created for my glory" Isaiah 43: 6-7

Every detail of our lives serves one purpose: to bring God glory. Does this mean God created us just to use us or so that he could become more glorious in Himself? No, rather, it means that God created us that His glory might be known and praised.

THE MASTER SCRIPT WRITER

Imagine being hired by God to be His scriptwriter for a day. Your first task would be to describe a life that brings us glory. What will you write? Let us say God wants to make a man the president of the world's strongest country. What will you write? How will the story add up?

Next, if you could write your story yourself, reflecting on how your life will give God glory, what will that story look like? I guess the first thing is that you will be born into the best family possible. Well, maybe I will include godly but definitely, I will include a very peaceful, loving, and wealthy family.

Interestingly, God has the best scripts. No human script can match His. Why? Our ways are not His ways. He weaves the stories of humans in an unimaginable way. If you doubt it, check out the story of Joseph or David. If you had met Joseph in the prison or Esther the orphan under the care of Mordecai, would you have imagined how their stories would end?

We are the *Josephs* and *Esthers* of our time. Our time in life is a bundle of stories. We all have a trail of events before our arrival and after we leave. Yes, the stories we have of ourselves today carve who we are, but it never entirely tells what trajectory our lives will take tomorrow.

The Sheikh of Dubai had a story he wanted to tell, an amazing blueprint he wanted to sell to the world about the beauty of his country. And on and on, that blueprint has become an edifice for the world to celebrate.

The big question is, how do we tell our stories? Can we trust ourselves to do a good job writing our stories? Well, for me, I don't. So, I leave it to the One who has the blueprint. I have chosen to follow His perfect plan in building my life.

If I had to continue writing my story without His interruptions, I guess it would probably read: Wura is a 'strong black woman' who was raised by her single mother. She is a good example of a talented, passionate, and goal-driven woman constrained by the Nigerian factor. She is an unmarried mother of 2 children and continues to lead a thriving group of 'scum' women.

I am forever thankful for His grace that brought my attention to His plans for a life built by God. Today, I am a thriving and fulfilled woman who continues to be a voice for a God-built life. My passion to work with women and children shows up in my research as a scientist. I lend my voice and self in every way possible to promote the beauty in the home led the way God designed it.

My story is meticulously spelled out in His blueprint, yours too. Every part of our stories fits perfectly into that blueprint. Our homes are only a chapter in that blueprint. What we know today isn't all there is about our lives. I look forward to upcoming amazing and glorious chapters in God's blueprint for my life. We live out our stories one way or another, some limiting and some empowering. I choose the latter.

How will I tell my story, the story of how I built my life? How will you tell yours?

REFLECTIONS

It's Time to Write a Story

You have done amazing work coming this far. At this point, I encourage you to take some time to write an amazing story about your life, looking over your shoulders into what has been and moving on gracefully onto what lies ahead.

We know the blueprints for our stories are found only in our Master Builder, God. Writing this story without Him is an exercise in futility. Therefore, take some moment to get on this journey with Him. You are welcome to start with this prayer:

Thank You, Abba:
For the gift of life,
For the amazing things You had in mind for me long before my birth,
For walking me through the journey of life,
For the many ways You look out for me.
As I spend my next moments of introspection in Your light,
Thank You for blessing me generously with Your presence.
Instruct and breathe upon my heart.
My mind is free of guile, resistance, wrong mindsets, or beliefs.
As I reflect, meditate, and put my thoughts to words,
I am still, and I hear Your voice.
In Jesus' name, Amen!

You saw me before I was born.
Every day of my life was recorded in your book.
Every moment was laid out
before a single day had passed- Psalms 139:16NLT.

What has your life's journey been? How did things fall apart? Put to words significant life experiences that have shaped who you are, right from childhood including the seemingly insignificant ones. If it comes to mind, then it is probably worth writing.

....

....

....

....

....

....

....

....

....

....

....

....

....

....

....

O LORD, you have examined my heart and know everything about me - Psalms 139:1 NLT.

In what specific ways do you think these events have shaped who you are today? Reflect on critical areas of your life and what ideals you hold on to. These areas include but are not limited to:

Identity and Self-Image

....

....

....

....

Love/Marriage/Significant Other

....

....

....

....

Career / Business / Calling

....

....

....

....

Friends / Associates

....

....

....

....

Financial Stability / Money

....

....

....

....

Health, Wellness and Fitness

....

....

....

....

Spiritual Growth and Development

....

....

....

....

Personal Growth

....

....

....

You know when I sit down or stand up.
You know my thoughts even when I'm far away- Psalms 139:2 NLT.

We travel light, in what areas have you experienced noteworthy disadvantages, hurts and negativity?

....

....

....

....

....

....

....

....

....

....

....

....

....

....

....

....

....

....

....

If I ride the wings of the morning, if I dwell by the farthest oceans, even there your hand will guide me, and your strength will support me- Psalm 139:9-10 NLT

What are your big needs, fears, and insecurities? Spend time matching up God's awesome strength with a scriptural verse and example that can be your anchor even as you begin to trust Him in each of these areas.

....

....

....

....

....

....

....

....

....

....

....

....

....

....

....

....

....

Search me, O God, and know my heart;
test me and know my anxious thoughts.
Point out anything in me that offends you,
and lead me along the path of everlasting life –
Psalms 139:23-24 NLT

God designed forgiveness not just for your offender but for you. In what ways do you need to forgive yourself? Who do you need to extend forgiveness to?

....
....
....
....
....
....
....
....
....
....
....
....
....
....
....
....

How precious are your thoughts about me, O God.
They cannot be numbered! I can't even count them;
they outnumber the grains of sand!
And when I wake up, you are still with me
– Psalm 139:17-18 NLT

Dreaming is free. Knowing you have all of the Master Builder's support and help, write about the next seasons of your life. His words and promises to us tell us Abba is poised to build beautiful stories and lives through us, what will that look like for you?

....

....

....

....

....

....

....

....

....

....

....

....

....

....

The Story of my Life

Abba, I am not a stranger to You
Rather, I am a daughter You know by heart,
A story that You never tire of telling or hearing.
A life that is familiar and dear to You, for You are its builder.
You see it all, my rising, my sitting, and my thoughts.
Long before I knew You, You knew me – having dreamed of me and planned my life.
You are my rock, my foundation, my pillar, immovable, unshakable, faithful, and fortress.
This knowledge alone brings me to my knees.
I have never known or seen love like this
The weight of Your love is a covering and although I don't understand it, I crave it.
Can I go away from Your Spirit?
Or escape your presence?
Truly, I have sometimes turned my heart away.
I have tried running;
hiding far into the comfort the world promises, sometimes lost in its travails.
But Your beautiful love is so unrelenting
When I turned my face away, You sought me and whispered love so sweetly.
When I sought darkness, You turned on the light.
When I tried to hide, You found me,

No matter how dark I thought my hiding place to be,
You found me.
You are light. To You, the night shines as bright as day.
You made me. You shaped the very core of my being
from deep within the mystery of the womb.
I honor You for Your workmanship. You have made
me unique.
You know every aspect of my frame since You formed
me in secret.
You looked across the expanse of time and saw me;
aware of all my days at that very time.
You had my specific design in mind right from the
start.
I'm always on Your mind. I matter to You! Your
precious thoughts about me are limitless.
Whether awake or asleep, You bless me with Your
presence
You stir wickedness out of my path
Examine me thoroughly, Father. Every inch of me.
Probe my thoughts and scrutinize my emotions.
And if You find anything that displeases You, please
lead me back to the path that brings me joy.

Psalm 139 (A paraphrase)
Adediwura Arowosegbe

SPECIAL NOTE

Dear One,

If you have come this far, you must have read through my story or you probably flipped through the pages of this book to this particular page. Does your story in any way sound similar to mine? Maybe not so similar, maybe a lot worse, or not so significant.

Your story no matter how far it has come is not entirely yours; it is one orchestrated by God and directed by Him if you'll allow Him. I pray that you find healing, hope, and strength as I found in God and that you go on building a beautiful life regardless of how storm-tossed your background is.

I'll love to remind you, once again, that even when it does not seem so, every part of your journey was carefully planned by the Master Builder. Nothing, not even the dysfunctionality of your home or upbringing disempowers God's plans for your life.

Parents,

Parenting is a call for two people to partner with God in raising a child. This call is already an enormous task for two people, let alone, one. If you are still navigating the storms for your marriage, here's praying that your home finds peace and healing.

Scriptures show that God consistently showed up for those forsaken by parents. I firmly believe God foreknew a season like this when you'll have to bear the responsibility of raising your kid(s) with one partner completely or partly out of the picture. He had you and your kid(s) in mind. No matter what, as long as you acknowledge and allow Him, God remains in this business of parenting with you.

Your struggles are seen and sacrifices acknowledged. I do not believe two parents can do it alone without God, let alone one. What makes the biggest difference is a partnership with God, the author of your kids' life – Depending and resting wholly on Him every single moment. He had the blueprint of our kids in His hands and He can bring all things together for His plans to come to fruition.

Friends and Family,

Thank you for investing in your loved ones by reading about their lives. You are a honored guest in this journey of ours. Thank you for reading about a life that you can only imagine and for cheering us on as we navigate this journey.

Connect:

I would love to hear from you, especially to know how this book has touched you. I'm happy to answer any questions you have as well.

Send an email to info@wuraarowosegbe.com to share your experience and questions from this book.

Do you want to be a part of an amazing youth community? Sign up to be a part of the *Built by Abba Youth Club*, a community I lead that encourages people to become their very best by acknowledging God's intentionality about their lives, no matter what they have been through. Sign up here:
bit.ly/builtbyabba

You can also join Building Beautiful Lives on Facebook, a community that is all about understanding and navigating through God intentionally towards building beautiful lives. This community is open to everyone and you can join here:
http://bit.ly/BuildingBeautifulLives

Are you a youth or young adult mentor? Please reach out to get this material at a discounted price for your young adults.

Thank you for journeying with me through the pages of this book.

Much Love,
Adediwura Arowosegbe

ABOUT THE AUTHOR

Fondly referred to as Abba's girl, Dr. Adediwura Arowosegbe is a speaker, writer and youth mentor. She is a crusader of the 'Built by Abba' message, spotlighting God as our life's master builder. She leads the Built by Abba Youth Club and Building Beautiful Lives online community, platforms that encourages people to become their very best by acknowledging God's intentionality about their lives, no matter what they have been through.

Wura is a researcher who loves to work with women and children. She advocates for improved care for mothers and their babies through her work with *Birth Counts*, a Maternal-Child Health Organization. Wura holds a Ph.D. in Medical Microbiology and Public Health from the Federal University of Agriculture, Abeokuta, Nigeria where she also spent some years lecturing undergraduate students. She is currently a graduate trainee at the University of Massachusetts Medical School, USA.

More about her on her website: www.wuraarowosegbe.com

Printed in Great Britain
by Amazon

61456666R00102